Even a Superhero Needs Counseling

What Superheroes and Super-villains Teach Us about Ourselves

Author of *When Parenting Backfires* and *The Modern Mystic*

Daniel Bates, LMHC

DB PRESS
Creative Endeavors That Matter

ISBN: 0-9973115-4-1
ISBN 13: 978-0-9973115-4-9
Library of Congress Control Number: 2016903120
LCCN Imprint Name: DB PRESS, Vancouver, Washington

Dedicated to comic books fans, nerds,

and psychology geeks everywhere.

Table of Contents

Introduction 1

Thanos 5

Thor.. 21

Spider-Man 33

The Punisher 43

Batman... 63

Superman... 75

Wonder Woman 85

Joker 93

Silver Surfer 107

Stephen Strange 119

Iron Man 131

Adam Warlock 143

Magneto.. 155

Gamora 169

Black Adam... 181

Scarlet Witch 195

Hulk 205

Spectre 217

Epilogue 231

Appendix A 233

About the Author 243

More from Daniel Bates 244

Podcasts and Blog from Daniel 252

Counseling Services...................................... 253

Introduction

I magine if you will, a devilishly handsome counselor (such as myself) sitting in his sophisticated-yet-welcoming counseling office, and wouldn't you know it, in walks Superman struggling with overwhelming anxiety. You can see the tears rolling down his beautifully chiseled face, his perfectly styled hair all tousled and messy. He's not even sure he wants counseling, but his wife, Lois, gave him an ultimatum: either he gets help or she's out. What would I do? How would I approach Superman's issues clinically? Well, wonder no longer! In this book, fantasy becomes reality.

I'm a licensed counselor and an avid comic book fan. This book combines my two passions into one tome. In the following chapters, I hypothesize what it would be like if a superhero or supervillain actually walked into my counseling office seeking help. In order to do that, I have to get into their psychology a bit. I dive into questions like: What makes them tick? What drives and motivates them? Why they became an antihero, superhero of villain? What kind of psychological issues are they struggling with? How might counseling help? And, most importantly, how are their stories and struggles instructive for your life.

You might think it's a bit odd to take life lessons from comic book characters, but is it really so odd? Some have argued that superheroes and super-villains are the modern equivalent of Greek gods and goddesses. They are cosmic projections of humanity's greatest fears, foibles, strengths and joys. They are gods of our own creation, divine beings created in our own image. As art imitates life, the gods imitate humanity. If true, comic book superheroes and super-villains act much like a mirror. They allow us to reflect upon our history, nature, condition and destiny. If a super-villain is ugly, it is because we are ugly. If a superhero is noble, it is because we are noble. Learning more about your favorite character will help you learn more about yourself. Comic books aren't just entertainment; they can be a window into you. They can be helpful on a practical level.

So if you love comics and want a deeper look into your favorite character, or you are interested in counseling and psychology, this is the book for you. You'll understand your favorite characters more and learn something about yourself.

Thanos

Thanos may be one of the most compelling and fascinating super-villains of the Marvel Universe. He is driven by a nihilistic worldview and desires the destruction of the universe, simultaneously overcome with an infatuation for Lady Death. He loves her obsessively. He tries with all his resources, scientific knowledge, advanced technology and power to feed her cravings for death. He lives to win her affection by feeding the gristmill of carnage. But what truly makes Thanos an interesting character is his drive for self-preservation. On several occasions Thanos teams up with odd bedfellows to fight for life. The first time, Thanos teams up with his enemy Adam Warlock to defeat Warlock's future alter-ego, the Magus. Thanos aided Warlock out of a desire to preserve the order of the universe and to eliminate a potential competitor to his power. The fight for life seems like an odd move given Thanos' power-hungry, nihilistic philosophy. This inner complexity is further illustrated post-*Infinity Gauntlet*, when Adam Warlock's other alter-ego, The Goddess, tries to eradicate all life in the universe. In this second episode, it is more obvious that Thanos is fighting for the preservation of life.

The third poignant and final episode happens after Thanos acquires omnipotence.[1] He is forced into a dilemma. The universe has a tear in the fabric of reality, one that cannot be mended despite his ultimate power. Thanos makes the choice to sacrifice himself for the sake of the universe. His death and relinquishing of power corrects the tear and allows life to continue.

This is confusing stuff given that we know Thanos is an ego-maniac. Why would Thanos sacrifice himself? The first place to start would be to examine the inner workings of his cognitive

---

[1] In *Infinity Gauntlet,* Thanos possesses ultimate power, but is defeated by Earth's superheroes. In *The End*, Thanos gains omnipotence without contest. He becomes the ultimate being in the universe.

landscape. Three main concepts define Thanos: Narcissism, Nihilism, and Co-Dependency.

Narcissism

Thanos is power-hungry. His ego feeds off a desire for control and suppression of others. He feels good when others look bad. You could make the argument that Thanos is a narcissist. He loves himself (excluding Lady Death) more than anyone else. He sees himself as being the most knowledgeable, most capable, powerful, intelligent being in the universe. None can compare with him. On several occasions, he has referred to himself as a god.

Narcissism is defined as "arrogant behavior, a lack of empathy for other people, and a need for admiration-all of which must be consistently evident at work and in relationships. People who are narcissistic are frequently described as cocky, self-centered, manipulative, and demanding. Narcissists may concentrate on unlikely personal outcomes (e.g. fame) and may be convinced that they deserve special treatment." [2]   As the definition indicates, narcissism is a personality disorder. That means it is not an acquired trait; it is innate to the person. In other words, Thanos was born with it; it is part of who he is. That also means it's an incredibly difficult thing to change. People who enter into counseling for the purposes of working on a personality disorder are in treatment for several years, and even then, there is no guarantee treatment will work.

For those in a relationship with narcissists, you know full well that the relationship exists for the purposes of the narcissist. This fits Thanos' profile. He uses people, situations and events like pawns in his ultimate scheme. The thoughts, wishes, feelings and values of others make little difference to him. He is the most important person in the relationship. His plans supersede other people. This is typical of the narcissistic personality disorder. Let's just say I wouldn't want Thanos on my caseload!

Additionally, beneath the appearance of confidence and self-esteem, the narcissist can be

---

[2]Psychology Today:
https://www.psychologytoday.com/conditions/narcissistic-personality-disorder. Retrieval: December, 27th, 2015.

incredibly insecure. If anyone questions their abilities, they fly into a rage. The very thought that someone could doubt them is incredible. Hmm... who does that sound like? Again, Thanos fits the bill. There are too many examples when an inferior questions Thanos' power, strength or plan, sending Thanos into a fit of indignation. He can't believe someone would doubt his power or cunning, which leads us to the final aspect of narcissism, aggression.

Narcissists are incredibly aggressive. They are aggressive in conversations, in getting jobs, in closing a sale, in promoting their work, idea or product. In some ways, this aggressiveness can be attractive. For the unsuspecting person, a narcissist's aggressiveness is winsome. They give the appearance of a go-getter, a fighter, a passionate person, which is all well and fine until that aggressiveness is turned against you. Therefore, don't get on Thanos' bad side.

Nihilism

Thanos was a nihilist to the very core. What does that mean? Nihilism is the view that any philosophical argumentation that life possesses value, meaning or purpose is patently false. All religious dogma, divine teaching or philosophical truth is null. This view is also characterized by extreme pessimism and extreme skepticism. A nihilist who takes his views seriously and tries to live them out would believe in nothing, refuse allegiance to anyone and anything, and ultimately seek destruction.

Friedrich Nietzsche, a German philosopher in the nineteenth century, is best known for his philosophy of existentialism and views on nihilism. He believed the force behind who determines the rules, creates morality and calls the shots is power. He called this the "will to power." Thanos might have been Nietzsche's greatest student. I'll get into some of the reasons why.

Thanos was "The last sons of A'Lars, progenitor of the second colony of the Eternals on Titan."[3] After Thanos murdered his mother and left Titan, he cruised the universe on a nihilistic murder spree. He used advanced technology, a crew of cosmic misfits, lethal weaponry, and enormous power to unleash a flood of destruction

---

[3] http://marvel.wikia.com/wiki/Thanos_(Earth-616). Retrieval: December, 28th, 2015.

for the sole purpose of destruction. He killed entire planetary populations for the fun of it. He believed there was no such thing as right and wrong, only subjugation and dominance. And he was the greatest of the latter. His nihilistic beliefs came into greater focus when he met Lady Death.

Co-Dependency

Death, Lady Death, or mistress Death was created when the universe was created. She is an abstraction personified in female form. She holds the power of decay and destruction. And she hungers for souls. However, her need is great and unsatisfied. Therefore, when Thanos falls in love with her, she is presented with an opportunity. She tolerates Thanos' overtures as a prize to be won if he kills enough people for her. Unfortunately for Thanos, love is an impossibility for Lady Death since she is an abstraction. He is addicted to a love she can't give, and she leads him on so that he meets her need for dead souls. The two are in a co-dependent relationship.

Co-dependency is defined as a dysfunctional relationship where two people use each other to meet their needs in an unhealthy way. Often, a co-dependent relationship can take the form of one person having an addiction, and the other person enabling that addiction. You can see the correlation with Thanos and mistress Death, right? Thanos is easily swayed by every whim of mistress Death. Her wish is truly Thanos' command. Mistress Death has an insatiable need for souls: you could call it an addiction. This isn't very dissimilar from addiction to alcohol, heroin or cocaine. People who are addicts often attract people who want to save them, but what often happens is that "saviors" become "enablers." Thanos is most certainly Lady Death's enabler. He feeds her addiction to death by unleashing wanton murder and destruction across the galaxy.

Was Thanos Really a Good Guy?

We've soundly rounded out the three defining characteristics of Thanos, but what about his character-breaking actions of teaming up with the good guys, saving the universe and ultimately sacrificing himself? When Thanos teamed up with Adam Warlock and other superheroes he didn't do it because he had a sudden change of heart. He didn't see the light and come over to the good side. Thanos was acting in his own self-interest. The threat of the Magus forced Thanos to pair up with the good guys to eliminate the common threat. That also holds true for when the Goddess was rising in her power. She was a competitor to Thanos' power. He didn't seek to destroy her for any moral reasons. He was only protecting his territory.

This brings us to the most contradictory action in Thanos' story, the sacrifice of his own life for the preservation of the universe. Once Thanos acquired omnipotence, he recognized that the fabric of reality was inalterably torn. The universe was off-balance and couldn't be rebalanced. The only option was hitting the reset button on the universe. Yet this posed a problem for Thanos. The only way he could hit the reset button was to sacrifice himself. One could not exist with the other. Faced with this inescapable dilemma, Thanos sacrificed himself so that the universe could continue. But did he do this for good purposes? Did he, at the end of all things, have a change of heart and become good? Frankly, it's unclear.

Thanos was also a pragmatist. Either he kept his power and everything ceased to exist (including Thanos) or, he would sacrifice himself and the universe continued. The cessation of existence, the destruction of everyone and everything is the goal of nihilism. Thanos, as I said earlier, is a nihilist. Yet, he doesn't hold on to power. Instead, he sacrifices himself, breaking with his philosophy so that reality carries on. Why does he do this? He sacrifices himself for pragmatic purposes. His sacrifice allows for the continuation of reality. And, as is true with most comics, Thanos' death wasn't really death at all. But more a death of his god powers.[4]

A side note. Personally speaking, there is a small part of me that views Thanos' actions as evidence for his good side. Maybe somewhere in his twisted thinking, power, pain and bloodlust was a change of heart. Many have argued that line of thinking summarized by statements like "Survival of the fittest," "Might makes right," and "Kill or be killed" is just cold logic. But can goodness have logical merit too? Can it be that "a rising tide lifts all boats"[5] manner of thinking is also logical? In that the good actions of one benefits the welfare of all, therefore, fostering

---

[4] Jim Starlin, *Marvel Universe: The End*, Marvel.
[5] The quote is taken from a speech President John F Kennedy gave in 1963.

goodness in yourself and in others ultimately benefits you.

Thanos' philosophy, his addiction to death, power, and intelligence all make him fearsome, but it is his character-breaking actions that make him interesting. He demonstrates the worst of humanity while also showing how humanity can change for the better. Change is possible even when faced with the limitations and harmful aspects of personality.

Therapy for Thanos

Where to begin? After building rapport with Thanos, I would highlight the incongruence between his dark philosophy and his good contradictory actions. This cognitive incongruity hopefully would stimulate some deep thought on Thanos' part. Psychologists call such incongruity *cognitive dissonance* (CD), the psychological state of acting in a way that conflicts with beliefs. For example, let's say you strongly believe in being fiscally responsible. But when you get online to shop, you spend frivolously. You say you love your wife, but when she makes you mad, you hit her. You want to live a clean and sober lifestyle, but when a craving hits, you relapse. See the disparity between belief and action? For many, this kind of incongruence is very uncomfortable. But there is hope if you struggle with cognitive dissonance. CD resolves in one of two ways: you change your beliefs to fit your actions, or change your actions to fit your beliefs. It is one or the other; there is no in-between. CD has a way of butting into your thoughts, nagging at you till the discrepancy is resolved. For Thanos, I would help him confront his discomfort.

Cognitive dissonance is a state that people avoid as much as possible. Yet, it is the elephant in the room. It is where people are typically stuck in their own personal development. If Thanos responded in the typical way, his cognitive dissonance would force him to seek some sort of resolution. At this point, I might appeal to his logical side, trying the angle that good presents a certain kind of inescapable logic. In this case, teaming up with heroes led to, as I said before, the preservation of his life, and not only his life but the life of the universe. And, what's good for the goose is good for the gander. By preserving life, Thanos preserves his power and dominion over others. What good is power if you have no one to exercise it over? What good is being an evil master if there is no one to serve you? Then I would offer an alternative. Let's say Thanos doesn't have to give up his power, but merely his evil practices. In other words, he can still be a dictator, just a benign dictator. And let's just say for fun, Thanos is intrigued by this thought. He's willing to give it some consideration. Not bad counseling, huh? I may have just saved millions of lives. You can thank me later.

Additionally, raising a person's awareness of their own cognitive dissonance can create a space where someone like Thanos could evaluate his personality, philosophy, and co-dependency. A fish in water is a useful analogy. Let's run a thought experiment; magically, a fish gains sentience and you can ask him questions. So, you ask him if it is wet being a fish. The fish gives you a funny look; he retorts, "What is wetness?" This may seem illogical, since the fish lives in water, but look at it from the fish's perspective. He *lives* in water. Water has become second nature to the degree that he doesn't even realize it's there. A human parallel to the fish's water could be culture. Culture shapes how we think, how we judge others and ourselves, what you think is "cool," how politics should run, and so on. However, you have no concept of how your culture has informed your worldview until you travel outside the culture, like a fish out of water. Okay, I may have mixed metaphors, but you get the idea. Personality is like water to a fish, or culture to a person who has never traveled. It is an unseen force that influences everything you do. Thanos has no idea there may be an issue in his personality causing problems. The same may be true for you, your co-worker, spouse or family member. If we are dealing with a personality issue, it may be very difficult for us to see it.

What is there to do? Is there any hope for someone dealing with a personality disorder like narcissism, or one with a skewed philosophy? Glad you asked (well I guess I did)! Cognitive dissonance creates an unavoidable "wall." You cannot pass through or over or under the wall until you deal with the wall itself. In other words, the wall is a crisis that forces a person to confront the problems of their personality or philosophy. For Thanos, his narcissism ran into a contradiction: he needed help from others to defeat the Magus and the Goddess. His nihilism ran into a contradiction: the destruction of the universe also meant the destruction of his self. And his co-dependency, which is another problem, ran into a contradiction: he was trying to win the love of someone who was never going to love him back. These are deep and powerful contradictions that anyone would avoid, but which must be addressed. Cognitive dissonance puts a stop to the avoidance and forces you to deal with these issues so that you can get resolution and move on with your life.

Are there areas in your life that you are avoiding? I would challenge you to stop running and finally face your cognitive dissonance. CD can be a prison of anxiety, self-doubt, and guilt for many. Stop living in denial. Face what you must face, even if that requires you to change your beliefs or your behavior. Living on the fence is no way to live.

Thor

God of Thunder, son of Asgard, brother of Loki and heir to Odin's throne: Thor is one badass superhero! But don't make the mistake that Thor has it easy. Beneath the male-model good looks, rippling muscles and godlike powers, the guy is working on a few things. If Thor walked into my counseling office looking for some help, how would I counsel him? Well, before I offer a diagnosis or advice, let's dive into his backstory first.

Thor is a man whose childhood could be considered by most a "charmed life." He was the golden child of Asgard. He was loved by his father, adored by his mother and worshiped by all those in the realm. But life wasn't perfect. Thor constantly battled with his brother in a sibling rivalry of cosmic proportions. Loki, Thor's adopted brother, was an abandoned Ice Giant baby. Odin took pity on the child and adopted him as his own. Even though Loki was taken in and considered an Asgardian, he never felt like he belonged. He felt an allegiance to the Ice Giants. And—did I forget to mention—he's conniving, mischievous, crafty and power-hungry? Loki wanted the Asgard throne and was keenly sensitive to the special attention given to Thor. He knew Thor was the chosen heir, but that didn't stop him from trying to get the throne for himself. It is important to understand the family dynamic. Thor's response to his brother's identity crisis reveals three things. Thor's poor response exposes and contributes to Loki's feelings of rejection and alienation. Second, we see more clearly Loki's desire for the throne. And finally, Thor's character is shown to be immature.

Thor, instead of showing compassion for his adopted brother, dismisses his pain. Put yourself in Loki's shoes for a moment. Loki is adopted, he's different, his powers aren't overtly impressive, and he doesn't feel like he belongs. That's a tough spot to be in. What does his brother Thor do? Thor both ridicules Loki's feelings and ignores them. Thor is so concerned with himself that he hardly notices his own brother's turmoil. As I said above, this reveals Thor's character to be lacking in quality. Young Thor is a gallivanting jerk, to use the proper clinical language. "Pride goeth before a fall" may have some applicability here. Yet, when Thor does fall, and he falls hard, we see the deepening of his character, the rounding out of his maturity, and a profound love for those under his protection.

The Fall

Odin was no dummy. He could see his son's pride, arrogance, and self-centeredness clearly. This troubled him greatly since he cared for the character of his son and the future of Asgard. Odin didn't want a selfish ruler on the throne. In order to teach his son a lesson, he removes his memories and places him in the body of Donald Blake, a partially disabled medical student living on Earth. Blake goes on to become a doctor and while on vacation in Norway encounters an alien scouting party. Blake retreats into a cave where he discovers Mjolnir, the mystical hammer of Thor.

The hammer transforms Blake into Thor, whereupon he defeats the aliens.

The story progresses with Blake and Thor as alter-egos. This allows Thor to find and fall in love with Jane Foster. More and more, Thor grows in his affection for the people of Earth. This is a formative time in Thor's life. Falling in love with Jane Foster was an act of disobedience towards his father. Odin exiled his son on Earth. However, from a counseling perspective, this is a positive step. Thor makes the decision not to live the life his father has preordained for him. He chooses his own path.

This choice becomes necessary when in parent-child relationship the child's life is subsumed by the parent's. The clinical term is *enmeshment*, the identity of the parent and child are entangled— there isn't a clear division between the parent and child's identity. This can, over time, create a toxic relational environment for both the child and parent.

For a large part of Thor's life, his goals were defined by his father. Odin and Thor were enmeshed. However, when Thor left for Earth, he abandoned Asgard because he didn't want to live the life his father created for him. He wanted to live his own life, pursue his own dreams and passions. When he broke with his father's expectations, this was a step in the right direction. Psychologists would term this *individuation*: this is another $10 psychology word.

Individuation is the act of disentanglement, of dis-enmeshment. Thor separated his identity from that of his father. And he struck out on his own. This is a magnificent thing. Imagine the alternative. Thor doesn't disentangle; he instead lives to fulfill the wishes of others. This can be developmentally and psychologically destructive because of the impact on identity. When a developing person isn't allowed to form their own identity outside of another like a parent they are emotionally immature, socially vulnerable, and cognitively unprepared to deal with the various demands of others in adulthood. It has been said "A man who stands for nothing will fall for anything." This quote illustrates rather poetically the problem with an under developed identity. If you don't know who you are, then you will be more easily swayed to follow the will of another person who may or may not have your best in mind. But this isn't the case for Thor. He separates his and his father's identity. He finds his own identity as a superhero and member of the Avengers, protector of Earth, and boyfriend to Jane Foster, not ruler of Asgard. Yet his story doesn't end there. There is a future for Thor and his father's relationship.

Individuation

After individuation, another development process follows, called *rapprochement*. This is the process by which the individuated child slowly returns to the relationship with their parent, but on a different footing. They return to the relationship with their parent as a peer. This is a far more stabilized form of relationship. Odin recognized the growth in Thor. He lifts the ban of Thor and restriction of Jane Foster. He allows Jane's entrance to Asgard. Odin even allows her to stay if she can pass a set of trials. Sadly, she doesn't pass the trials, but this does show Odin's effort to connect with his son on a peer-to-peer level. Thor and Odin reestablish their relationship, but Thor still has no interest in taking his father's throne. Just when things are getting good between Thor and his father, Thor faces his greatest tragedy. Enter stage left: Surtur.

Surtur, a fire demon, has been constructing for thousands of years "Twilight," the Sword of Doom. This sword is all-powerful. The demons used the sword in a cosmic battle between him and Odin. Surtur weakens Odin and drags him into a rift. This rift is forever sealed and it is presumed that Odin died. Thor is, understandably, destroyed by the loss of his father. This leaves an inescapable hole in Asgard that must be filled. Thor still won't take the throne, yet he steps up to the plate and fights off Hela, reconnects with his great-grandfather, Tiwaz, and foils a nefarious plot of Loki's design. The immature Thor would have likely ignored these battles and responsibilities, but the new and matured Thor meets these challenges head on.

Further evidence of his personal growth is shown by his teaming up with Loki to fight off an attack from the Ice Giants. The Ice Giants try to kill Thor by finding the Midgard Serpent, but instead awaken the dragon Fin Fang Foom. This initiates a cascade of events that eventually enables Thor to rescue his father, Odin.

Therapy for Thor

Knowing what I know, I would recommend Thor finally bury the hatchet with his brother. For you comic book fans, you know that after Thor rescues his father, he kills his brother. Geez, Thor! I didn't mean *literally* "bury the hatchet." Thor needs to learn how to exist in relationship with difficult people. That means forgiving those who have hurt him the most. It also means asking for forgiveness.

Yes, Loki is deceitful, scheming and power-hungry, but at one point he was a hurting brother needing support. Thor blew his brother off. That hurts. Yes, Thor was arrogant, self-centered, and was only concerned about himself, but he did save Loki on several occasions and he has matured. These two brothers need to reconcile, and that can only begin with forgiveness. Here are my forgiveness ABC's for Thor and Loki and for you too.

- **A—Acknowledge:** This first step entails bringing the grievance to the other person's attention. But you aren't simply focused on the single incident. You are focusing on the pattern. So if your spouse is repeatedly disrespectful to you when making decisions, share that you see a pattern and that pattern hurts you. It causes damage to your communication, and you'd like it to stop. Your goal is to be honest, but don't attack the other person. That will put them on the defensive and will shut down the communication process. You are sharing because you want the best for them and for the relationship.

- **B**—Begin to Process: The goal of this step is to share the *what, why* and *how*. The other person ought to listen in order to understand. You ought to share not so that you can be right and rub the pattern in the other person's face. You are sharing for the purposes of the other person's growth. You are sharing so that they can understand the pattern and how it has affected you.

- **C**—Commit: This is the point at which you can share specifics of what the other person can do to make things better. For the other person, they need to listen carefully and commit to new behaviors, attitudes and mindsets that are healthier. This step should also include your commitment to supporting them in their growth. Change can only happen when you work together.

This is a relational focus for Thor. Aside from past immaturity, it is his relationships that need work. He and Odin have gone through the process of enmeshment, individuation, and rapprochement leading to Thor's maturation. Yet, Thor and Loki still have some work to do. I would recommend Thor bring his brother to one of the sessions if he's willing. Then I would sit both of them down and walk them through the ABC's of forgiveness. Confronting each other and working through forgiveness is not an easy thing to do, but it's worth the pain. The process is full of missteps. However, if both parties can listen to each other empathetically when feelings do arise, acknowledge what they did, understand how it hurt the other person and commit to making things better, the relationship will heal.

I recognize this is a recommendation for fictional characters forgiving each other and moving on, but it seriously can work for you. This is a process I walk real-life clients through. If you have difficult people in your life, don't just ignore the hurts that have transpired. Have a courageous conversation with them. Face what happened and engage in the forgiveness ABC's. Be ready to ask for forgiveness or, share how you have been wounded by the other. If they care enough to listen, they may be willing to follow the ABC's with you. It's uncomfortable, but forgiveness is necessary for relationships to move forward.

Spider-Man

Your friendly neighborhood Spider-Man to the rescue! What's going on? My Spidey-Sense is going off the charts! I think someone is in emotional distress.

The character and the story of Spider-Man possess appeal and relatability, unlike any other superhero stories. Speaking personally, Spider-Man connected with me when I was a kid. I could relate to feeling like an outcast, but wanting to fit in; having a secret love for a girl, but not knowing how to express it; having a vivid imagination, but feeling like my life was going nowhere; wounded by family tragedy, but wanting to move on. But unlike myself, Peter Parker had the opportunity to escape the painful paradoxes of his life when bit by a radioactive spider. He was able to live out the fantasy I wanted and I'm sure every other 12-year-old boy wanted it too. Needless to say, Spider-Man is a *tour de force* of relatability. It's no wonder that Spider-Man had such broad appeal to a young, male demographic.

Even though Peter Parker was able to escape his life when he became Spider-Man, his life wasn't perfect. Being a superhero brought even more paradoxes into Peter's life. He tried his best to juggle an intimate relationship with Mary Jane while living up to the standard that Uncle Ben gave him—"With great power comes great responsibility." Not to mention, the extreme danger that came along with being a superhero. Yet, in that struggle between managing two identities, Spider-Man maintains a sense of humor. (As a side note, Sigmund Freud considered humor the highest defense mechanism. Sometimes it works to laugh off your pain.)

If Spider-Man swung into my office looking for help, what advice would I give? Well, let's collect some background data first. The storyline of Spider-Man is sprawling. The reason is that the Spider-Man franchise has so many iterations, it's hard to keep track. And once you add multiple dimensions into the mix then there's trying to figure them all out. There is the "Amazing Spider-Man," "The Spectacular Spider-Man," or "Friendly Neighborhood Spider-Man." Then you have to consider the "Secret Wars" and all the crossovers. To cover Spider-Man's entire background story would be too much for this book. Therefore, I'll discuss the *The Amazing Spider-Man* narrative, considered by many to the be authoritative Spider-man story.

A Brief History of Peter Parker and Spider-Man

Peter Parker's parents were tragically killed when he was young. His Aunt May and Uncle Ben took him in. They raised him as if he were their own son. They loved him dearly. As Peter became a teenager, it was obvious he had a gift for academics, especially in science, but he struggled socially. All of that was about to change. One day, when Peter attended a science exhibit, he was bitten by an irradiated spider. Quickly, Peter realized he had newfound power akin to a spider. He could climb walls, sense danger, and had superhuman strength. Peter decided to enter a televised wrestling contest to test out his newfound powers. He won easily and impressively. This made him an overnight sensation. Succored by his new fame and money, he created the Spider-Man costume and web shooters. One night, enamored with himself and indifferent to the plight of others, he let a petty thief escape the wrestling club. This would be a fateful decision. After being away several days, Peter returned home to learn of his beloved Uncle Ben's murder. Peter tracks down the killer and to his horror, realizes the killer was the thief he allowed to escape from the wrestling club. Wracked with guilt, Uncle Ben's words—"With great power comes great responsibility"—hit him like a truck. He had the power to stop what eventually lead to Uncle Ben's death, but he had done nothing. Never again would he squander his powers; and thus, Spider-Man was born. From there, Peter dedicated his life to living with a purpose. He used his power for the benefit of others.

Okay, yes, there's a lot more to the storyline, such as falling in love with Gwen Stacy, Gwen's murder at the hands of Peter's best-friend-turned-arch-enemy, Harry Osborn, meeting, falling in love with and marrying Mary

"This brings us to..."

Jane, joining the Avengers, and (not to mention) clones and multiple dimensions (yeah, latter Spider-Man gets kind of weird). But I want to focus on the core of the story. Peter's life is marked by a process of personal growth, loss and resiliency. He is an example of someone who lives his life with purpose.

A Page out of Spidey's Playbook

This brings us to, quite possibly, the greatest superpower Spider-Man possesses. Every time a dream is crushed, he carries on. He models the spirit of resiliency. Even though Uncle Ben died tragically, his message impacted Peter in such a way as to give his life a goal. This is what enabled him to endure so many trials. His strength came from his purpose.

What about you? What purpose are you living for? What drives you? What gets you excited? Are you living in a way that is congruent with your life purpose? If you're unhappy with your life, this is a line of inquiry worth following. Take a page out of Spider-Man's playbook and live life with a purpose.

Spider-Man and Grieving

The brilliance of Stan Lee and all the numerous writers who worked on the Spider-Man storyline is seen in their making Spider-Man so human. How did they do this? They allowed us to see him struggle. And not just struggle against a super-villain in battle, but struggle with very personal things. Many times we see Spider-Man run away from his problems. He, like most of us, I'm sure, is afraid of facing loss. The death of Uncle Ben, Gwen Stacy, Aunt May, and the temporary disappearance of Mary Jane are horrible events. We, like Spider-Man, all face tragic losses. Yet our resilience is founded on our ability to grieve.

Loss, change, and grief are normal aspects of life. Life is not about avoiding these things, but engaging with them. Unfortunately, not many of us know how to engage with grief in a healthy and positive way. Psychologist William Worden gives us a way. He divides healthy grieving into four tasks. These aren't "stages," which would imply that we are passively carried through grief. Instead, Worden conceptualizes grief as a "task." He means it is something that will require effort, work and personal and emotional engagement. The four tasks are:

- **Task 1: Accept the Reality of the Loss:** You must confront your own denial that part of your life is gone. Your life has changed and that's okay. You can't move until you face reality.

- **Task 2: Experience the Pain of Grief:** For whatever reason, we are afraid to feel in our culture. We take pills, distract ourselves with entertainment and generally avoid discomfort, but this is not helping us. This avoidance of feel grief is compounding our pain. Experience the pain of what you have lost. It is the only way for you to accept the reality of what has happened.

- **Task 3: Adjust to an Environment:** Life is not the same now that your marriage has ended, your friend has moved away or that your work has laid you off. You must find a new "normal." Don't try to recreate what you had. Take what's in front of you and work with that.

- **Task 4: Embark on a New Life:** Even though that part of you is gone and irretrievable as a result of the change, it is still of who you are. Memories are the foundation of your identity. You cannot keep your parent, child, career or dream physically alive through maintain their memory. Rather, the memory that you do have is not one of pain, but of joy, wisdom, and comfort. What you lost can guide you to future successes. Loss and failure can be a stepping stone to accomplishing your dream.

If Spider-Man were in my counseling office, I would walk him through these four tasks. The worst thing Spider-Man could do is to allow the losses in his life to effectively end his life. Spider-Man has overcome so much adversity. To allow these losses to end his story would be the ultimate tragedy. Yet the avoidance of healthy grieving is like putting one foot in the grave.

What are the benefits of healthy grieving? What are the disadvantages of avoiding grief? Healthy grieving allows you to move forward. But too many want the "moving forward" part without the hard work. That "cheap" kind of moving forward isn't really moving forward at all. It's more ignoring and avoiding, which actually accomplishes the opposite of moving forward. It instead keeps you stuck.

Cheap moving forward cements you where you are. Physically, you are getting older, you kids will grow and the place you live in may change, but inside, you are still in that same place. Moving forward isn't cheap; it will cost you something. You will have to face painful things. You'll have to accept what is no more. You will have to engage in the four tasks of grief. But, the payoff is the ability to move forward. So you have to ask yourself, "Is the cost of moving forward worth it?" I would argue it is.

If Spider-Man approached me for counseling, I would suggest that he must face the loss of Uncle Ben, Gwen and Aunt May. He must engage in the work of grieving. It is the only way he can move forward. Grieving is not about forgetting those you've lost. However, the absence of that person doesn't inhibit the progress of your life. You can continue with life knowing the gift of the time you had with them, drawing strength and courage from their memory.

I would also point out that Spider-Man is more than capable of accomplishing the tasks of grieving. He overcame so much in his past. Spider-Man knows from experience he can do it. If you ignore an enemy, you leave yourself open to attack and defeat. The best course of action is to address the issue head-on. Spider-Man would do no less if he were facing Doctor Octopus, the Green Goblin, Venom, Carnage, or the Sandman. Grieving is no different. Take a page out of Spider-Man's playbook and engage with the work of grieving. Address the losses in your life. If you don't, you put yourself in a vulnerable position. Just because you cannot see an enemy doesn't mean they aren't there. Be resilient and do the hard work of grieving. Then, and only then, can you move forward with your life.

The Punisher

He may be on the side of the angels, but you don't want to get on the Punisher's bad side. Born in Queens, New York, Frank Castle (born Castiglione) entered seminary to become a priest. But Frank was faced with an ultimate moral dilemma: How can God forgive those who committed evil acts? How could he forgive those who are evil? Because of this internal conflict, Castle chose to leave his studies, he got married and entered the United States Marine Corps. Castle trained as, among other things, a sniper, and served in the Vietnam War. He won several medals for his valor and skill as a soldier. He returned home from the war to resume life with his wife and children in New York City. And this is where things get ugly.

One day Castle was out with his family in Central Park having a picnic. The pleasant family outing was violently interrupted when Frank and his family witness a mafia execution. Wanting to erase any witnesses, the Costa crime family killed any witnesses to their crime, including Frank's whole family. But Frank survived. And Frank wasn't happy.

Castle assisted the police in identifying all his shooters but, due to corruption within the department, the killers were never brought to justice. Not able to forgive, wanting justice and feeling betrayed by the justice system, The Punisher was ready to enter Castle's life. Castle decided to take justice into his own hands and kill the men who did him wrong. Castle assumes the identity of the Punisher and wages a one-man war against any and all criminals. He exacts a lethal form of justice not many superheroes could justify.

Frank is a unique superhero in that he isn't your typical superhero at all; he's an antihero. He uses the methods and means of criminals, those whom he detests, to bring about good ends. He is a walking example of "the ends justifying the means." However, his practices lead to his ostracism from the superhero community. He's considered a rogue. He blurs the line between "good guy" and "bad guy." This blurring is most dramatically portrayed in the comic *Original Sin*. In this story, Nick Fury has been conducting a secret mission outside of his S.H.I.E.L.D. duties, a secret mission that absolutely no one knows about. The mission? To be Earth's assassin. Nick Fury is the man on the wall—the wall being a metaphor for the barrier between Earth and malicious, imperialistic alien forces desiring the destruction or subjugation of Earth.

According to Fury, he's defended Earth innumerable times using deadly force. However, Fury is getting along in years. Fury created a crisis, the death of the Watcher, as a kind of test to determine who would be his replacement. Among the candidates were The Punisher and the Winter Soldier. Ultimately, the Winter Soldier won out, since The Punisher would likely be too *gung-ho* about killing. The Winter Soldier was willing to be lethal, but was more reserved in his decisions to kill. The job description required some discretion. Castle too much liked killing anything he considered a threat. He didn't get the job; sorry, Frank!

Castle's over-enthusiasm for killing is showcased in Marvel's *Civil War* storyline. Captain America is building up his numbers in opposition to Iron Man and government registration of all superheroes. They considered enlisting The Punisher after he saved a badly beaten Spider-Man, yet Captain America struggled with the choice. His skills were exactly what the underground cause needed, yet his presence on the team compromised their moral stance. Captain America allowed him to join, but Frank later killed two criminals also wanting to join, and Cap booted him, regretting that he ever let him in.

If ever Frank, reconsidering his life choices, slowed down on his quest for revenge and walked into my office asking for counseling, I'd first make him relinquish all weapons. I'm not stupid. But, based on his story, I'd offer up some advice that I think could really help Frank.

PTSD and Punisher

I think it's safe to assume Castle may be suffering from Post-Traumatic Stress Disorder. Think about it. Castle is a veteran of the Vietnam War.

He witnessed the murder of his wife and kids and had to suffer the injustice of a corrupt police department. Yes, I think it's very safe to say that Castle has serious trauma in his life. What does PTSD look like, how does it affect people, and what could Punisher do to get help?

PTSD occurs when someone is exposed to a fear-inducing situation, but once the situation is over, the person still feels the effects of that fear. For example, you get into a nasty car wreck. Some guy is drunk while driving and drifts into your lane, hitting you head-on. You survive with some serious physical injuries which heal, but the psychological damage persists. You begin having nightmares about the accident; every time there's a banging sound you jump out of your skin, and you refuse to get in a car. But that is just one example. PTSD can result from any number of traumatic experiences, like being mugged, kidnapped, raped, shot, bombed, like surviving earthquake, flooding, or abuse, or like witnessing a loved one experience such trauma. Many veterans suffer from PTSD. They were the first population shedding light onto the disorder.

PTSD has three main characteristics:

- Re-experiencing symptoms in the form of flashbacks, bad dreams, and frightening thoughts.
- Avoidance of emotional triggers like staying away from things that remind you of the trauma, which can lead to feeling numb, feeling guilt, and depression.
- Hyper-arousal, like being easily startled, on edge, having trouble sleeping and being prone to angry outbursts.

One could hypothesize that each time Castle encounters a criminal he gets triggered. "Trigger" is a useful term for a thing that initiates said symptoms. In Castle's case, it's easy to see how he could get triggered, causing him to have a flashback. He feels overwhelming guilt that he couldn't protect his family; has an angry outburst, resulting in the killing of a criminal. Could this happen in real life?

Yes, and no. A person with PTSD gets triggered and struggles with said symptoms daily. It is very rare, though, for a triggered person with PTSD to become lethal. The story of Chris Kyle comes to mind. He was one of the most decorated officers—and is considered one of the most, if not the most, lethal snipers—in American military history. He was also the subject of a recent Clint Eastwood movie, *American Sniper*. After Kyle was honorably discharged, he was struggling. The movie vividly portrays Kyle experiencing some of the symptoms of PTSD. Thankfully, he finds his footing. Kyle starts helping out other veterans. This was his saving grace and, ironically, the cause of his death. One day, Kyle and his friend, Chad Littlefield, took another veteran, Eddie Ray Routh, out to a shooting range. Routh was struggling with PTSD as well. While at the shooting range, Routh killed Kyle and Littlefield. Police found the two men with their guns holstered, safety on, and no rounds fired. They were killed without warning. I share this story not to instill fear of veterans, but to highlight the gravity of PTSD. Routh later shared his sorrow for what he did. It's also important to mention that Routh had been diagnosed with Schizophrenia.

This raises the question, are veterans, or anyone suffering from PTSD, dangerous? The answer is complicated. Yes, there have been crimes, and even mass shootings, committed by veterans. Yet, it is hard to say they did this because of the PTSD. Let's take a look at the Fort

Hood mass shootings in 2009 and 2014. The 2009 shooting was committed by a military psychiatrist, of all people. Major Nidal Hasan shot and killed 13 people, and wounded 30. It is unknown why he committed the shooting, but some hypothesize he was radicalized (he was a Muslim) and had underlying mental health issues. The 2014 shooting was committed by Ivan Lopez-Lopez. He was suffering from PTSD. He killed three. Lopez had several complaints, one being that the military made it difficult for him to attend his mother's funeral. There are many other cases of veterans being violent and committing crimes. PTSD and other mental health issues are often characterized as making someone violent or criminal; however, they are not causative of violent or criminal behavior. PTSD is one factor among many that could make someone violent.

Researchers [6] have investigated this question and found that PTSD does contribute to violence and criminal behavior. Yet, it is a correlational, and not causative, relationship. And it is one factor among others, such as history

[6] APA PsychNET:
http://psycnet.apa.org/index.cfm?fa=buy.optionToBuy&id=2012-26670-001#. Retrieval: January, 30th, 2016.

of violence, presence of intense irritability, struggles with anger and emotional outbursts, lack of social support, homelessness or joblessness. The more risk factors involved in someone's life, the higher likelihood of violence and criminal behavior.

Given that PTSD can contribute to violence and crime coupled with the fact that veterans have a higher incidence of PTSD than the general population should not evoke fear, but our sympathy. We, as a nation, need to understand PTSD better and have compassion on our military men and women. These people were willing to make the ultimate sacrifice for our safety and freedom. We owe them more than what they receive. They deserve our help, understanding, and compassion. The same goes for non-veteran sufferers of PTSD: the way we ought to respond is not with fear, but with support. The person struggling with PTSD is a human being who has seen the worst life can offer. What they need more than anything is compassion.

Fortunately, PTSD is a treatable condition. Through a combination of talk therapy, medication and support groups, veterans and other PTSD sufferers manage their symptoms and find healing. There is help out there. Don't suffer in silence. Seek help! Or, if your loved one is suffering from PTSD, compassionately encourage them to join a support group, get counseling and see a psychiatrist for medication.

Impulse Control or Values

The Punisher isn't naive. He knows the moral implications of killing criminals without due process. One can only surmise either that he doesn't care, or that he can't stop himself. Either case is problematic, right?

If indeed he has stopped caring, we indeed need to be worried. Captain America rightly identified this concern in *Civil War*. The problem is, when The Punisher takes the law into his own hands, he can be wrong. Yes, it can feel instantly gratifying when a criminal gets what they deserve, but this feeling appeals to our baser nature, the desire for vengeance. Vengeance is a slippery slope. It can drive people to make terrible decisions. Punisher's whole life is driven by vengeance. That opens him up to making serious mistakes. He can make rash judgments; he's not impartial. He can act based on bias. Therefore, it's entirely possible he exacts lethal justice unjustly. Like I said before, don't get on his bad side. For example, if the Punisher mistakes you for a criminal, you're dead. No *ifs*, *ands* or *buts*: you're dead. If you are falsely accused of a crime you didn't commit, there's no investigation, no weighing of the evidence: you're dead. Or, let's say, you're not a criminal, but you are perceived as a threat to the Punisher: again, you're dead. Do you see the problem?

On the other hand, what if the Punisher does care about justice and due process, but he simply can't stop himself? Psychologists would classify this as an *Impulse Control Disorder* (ICD). For a frame of reference, disorders in this classification include eating disorders, compulsive gambling, kleptomania, trichotillomania, intermittent rage disorder, pyromania, compulsive shopping, compulsive skin picking, and compulsive risky sexual behavior. That list should give you a sense of what impulse control disorders are like. The short definition of ICD is an addiction to a behavior. In other words, it's an addiction not to a substance, but to an action. Castle may be addicted to the act of killing. If this is true, how can he justify killing under the auspices of justice? This is where we get a little Freudian.

In psychoanalysis, there is a concept called *sublimation*. Sublimation is the process by which someone takes a socially unacceptable desire, like taking pleasure in beating people, and turns it into a socially acceptable activity, like boxing. This is what Castle has done in order to live with himself. He is a man of principle, but he also has a love for killing. In order to meet his need while living in accordance with his moral code, he justifies his actions by restricting his killing to criminals. Freud actually considered sublimation a higher-order defense mechanism and thought it was a sign of maturity. Kudos, Punisher! Freud approves of you!

Treatment for Impulse Control

If Frank walked into my counseling office seeking help with his impulse control problem, I would take a three-pronged approach. First, I would use a Cognitive-Behavioral Therapy (CBT) approach for our talk therapy. CBT is a model of psychotherapy developed by psychologist Aaron Beck. In short, the goal of CBT is to expose and examine hidden beliefs and assumptions that influence one's view of self, others and the world. Beliefs can be grounded in reality, healthy and stable, or they can be divorced from reality, unhealthy, and unstable. The latter category causes all sorts of mental health problems. It is the therapists job to assist clients in challenging those unhealthy beliefs for the purpose of substituting new ways of thinking that match reality and are healthy.

Frank has a few assumptions that I would help him examine, test and substitute. For example, Frank puts people in overly simplistic categories of good or bad. He also believes that the justice system is fundamentally broken, therefore, the only way to get justice is to exact it himself. Additionally, he believes he will never have peace until all the culprits of his family's death have been killed. With each belief mentioned above, we would:

- **Identify Beliefs— Cognition.** I would listen carefully to Frank's story and then feed back to him what his beliefs are that guiding his behavior, for example "People are either good or bad," "Justice system doesn't work so I'll get justice for myself," and "There is no peace until all culprits of my family's death are killed."

- **Recognize Outcomes of Beliefs-Behavior.** What Frank believes determines his behavior, for example, if he believes someone fits in the "bad" category, he kills them without equivocation or remorse. He behaves this way because he believes the justice system doesn't work.

- **Examine Beliefs and Outcomes Against Personal Values- Feeling.** Frank considers himself a "good" guy. He does what he does because he wants to right a wrong. However, his methods have had bad outcomes, good people have been hurt as a result of his actions. And his killing has extended far beyond his mission to right the wrong of his family's death. He's a risk of becoming what he despises, a cold-blooded killer. Weighing his actions against his feelings and values ought to create an internal conflict.

- **Test or Challenge Beliefs- Substitution.** Recognizing the internal conflict mentioned above creates an opportunity for Frank to challenge his previously held beliefs and test them against other beliefs. I'd start by having him find counter arguments to his beliefs like: examples of bad people doing good things, examples where the justice system works, and people finding a peaceful resolution and healing after the loss of their family. Then, based on this new information, what new, more accurate, beliefs could Frank substitute for his old, inaccurate, beliefs? Frank could accept the fact that people are complicated and don't always fit overly simplistic categories. He could accept that the justice system, for all its flaws, does exact justice in many instances. Finally, he could come to grips with the loss of his family, begin to heal and move on.

Walking Frank through these four steps, it is likely his impulsivity would drop. He'd think twice before "offing" someone. He might look for legal means to bring about justice. He might, instead of avoiding the loss of his family by way of carrying out a mission of vengeance, deal with his feelings of sadness and grief.

Second, the research study I referred to earlier found that PTSD in combination with extreme irritability can be a dangerous catalyst. If that's true, therapy would primarily focus on stress-reduction techniques that can help Frank mediate stress-inducing situations. I would teach Frank four Stress-Reduction Techniques:[7]

- The first stress-reduction technique is progressive muscle relaxation. It involves a seven-second tightening and releasing of specific muscle groups from head to toe, with emphasis on noticing the difference between the tense feeling and the relaxed feeling.
- The second technique is learning how to release muscle tension without first tensing the muscles. This is done by focusing attention on the muscles and visualizing the tension being released.
- The third technique is cue-controlled relaxation, in which a person is taught to relax his or her body by saying a relaxing word, such as "peace" or "relax," with each slow exhalation.

---

[7] PsychSolve: https://www.newharbinger.com/psychsolve/impulse-control-disorders. Retrieval: January, 30th, 2016.

- And, finally, the fourth technique is special-place visualization. This skill teaches the person to envision a place of safety and comfort in his or her imagination. The person can go to this "mental safe place" whenever he or she is overwhelmed by distressing feelings.

Second, I would have Frank see a psychiatrist and get on some medication. People often confuse the title psychiatrist with psychologist. The professions are actually quite different. A psychiatrist is a medically trained doctor who specializes in the treatment of mental health disorders. Psychiatrists don't typically practice "talk therapy," although some do. Generally, psychiatrists perform short interviews to evaluate, diagnose, prescribe, and monitor the effectiveness of psychotropic medications. On the other hand, psychologists are not medically trained, they are not doctors and they do not prescribe medications. They are strictly trained in psychological assessment, diagnosis and treatment of mental health disorders. Getting back to Frank, there are effective psychotropic medications that can help people struggling with PTSD. Psychiatrists have a number of medications at their disposal to help someone with depression, anxiety, insomnia, and impulsivity, which are the primary symptoms of PTSD.

It is important for someone like Frank to see his psychiatrist regularly since there is some art to the science. Sometimes medications won't work because of client's individual metabolic, psychological, and dietary issues. Therefore, psychiatrist can change dosage, medication combinations, and types of specific drugs in order to find the right prescription for a client. I would strongly encourage Frank to regularly see his psychiatrist since clients often drop out when the drugs don't initially work. But, just because a drug didn't work initially doesn't mean it won't work at all. Unfortunately, mental health sufferers don't often give psychiatry a chance since their expectations may be unrealistic. They may want an instant fix which medications can't do. It takes time, depending on the drug, for it to reach its full effectiveness in the body. And, it takes time to find the right dosage, medication combination, and type of drug that works just right for the client. Yet, when clients can stay the course and work with their psychiatrist, they tend to have the best outcomes.

Third, I would have Frank attend weekly support group meetings with other Veterans. Being around other people who have similar backgrounds and struggles can be very powerful. This three-pronged approach is effective for people struggling with PTSD, addiction or impulse control disorders.

For someone just coming to grips with their PTSD, diagnosis, treatment and recovery may seem overwhelming. Overcoming PTSD may feel like an unreachable goal. Rid yourself of this thought. Every day there are people who cope, manage and succeed in their fight with PTSD. It is not a death sentence. There is hope.

Batman

The Caped Crusader, the Dark Knight, the Bat, whatever you want to call him—the world of comics is incomplete without Batman. Why is Batman so cool? Does that question even need to be asked? A better question: how is he *not* cool? First of all, Bruce Wayne is a total stud. He has tons of money, he's suave and good looking. He's also super smart and smooth with the ladies. His butler, Alfred, is totally cool and sarcastic. Oh, and did I mention, he moonlights as a superhero. Probably the coolest thing about Batman is that he's not a superhero at all. That is, Batman has no superhuman powers. Yes, he is buff. Yes, he is smart. Yes, he is the world's greatest detective. And yes, he is rich and has tons of cool gadgets, but no superpowers to speak of. But what Batman lacks in superpowers, he makes up for in drive, leadership and intelligence. Plus, he has great combat skills amplified by advanced technology.

The Good

Batman, like I said above, has three fantastic qualities. First off, he has drive like no other superhero, or super-villain, for that matter. In fact, in *Final Crisis* when Darkseid is trying to take over Earth, he kidnaps Batman and uses a super-villain by the name of "The Lump" to probe Batman's mind in an attempt replicate his psyche in a batch of super-soldiers. These super-soldiers would possess the guile, determination, and resourcefulness of Batman, but would do so in service to Darkseid. Yet, the plan is foiled. When Batman's consciousness is transferred to The Lump, he finds a way to mentally overwhelm his enemy and free himself.

Second, Batman is a leader. Readers often see him together with Superman at the helm. Together, they provide the superheroes with leadership for whatever crisis that befalls the Earth. This isn't just good story, it also demonstrates something rather profound: the limitations of superheroes. They may have super-strength, heightened senses, the ability to control matter, super-speed, and all that—but when it comes to decision making, well, they're in the dark just like the rest of us. There is no "superhero manual." Their decisions can have serious consequences. They aren't immune from being wrong, even when they mean well. That's why Superman needs Batman, and vice-versa. They offer a counterbalance to each other. They can challenge each other's thinking and choices. They also offer up unique perspectives. Superman has the ability to unite superheroes together for one cause. Batman offers his incredible deductive abilities for analyzing the motives and plans of the criminal mind, and most importantly, a stratagem for taking villains down. Think of Batman as a modern-day Sherlock Holmes with more social adeptness and money.

Third, Batman is one smart dude. I alluded to this above, but Batman is a really smart guy assisted by advanced technology. In fact, Bruce Wayne is one of the richest superheroes in the DC universe. This allows him to funnel massive amounts of money into the creation of advanced crime-fighting technology. Furthermore, he has incredible deductive abilities. In other words, he thinks like a detective. This is good, but the fact that he can think like a criminal is even better. He can do this not only because he's logical, but also because he's empathetic. Empathy, quickly defined, is the ability to understand another person's motives, reasoning, and worldview. Batman can empathetically understand a criminal. Doesn't mean he agrees with them or approves of what they do, but he can understand them. Look out, criminals!

The Bad

The dark side of the Dark Knight is well... pretty dark. Bruce witnessed the death of his two parents at a very early age. This robbed Bruce of having a family. And his wealth isolated him from the stresses and supports of normal life. He was effectively an orphan, completely alone except for Alfred. Growing up in isolation—without the love, support and tenderness of a caregiver—can have serious implication for a child's development.

Losing one's primary caregiver early on, like in the case of Bruce Wayne, can affect a person's attachment style. To explain, in the 50's and 60's, researchers discovered that disruption to the relationship between a child and their primary caregiver had long-lasting effects. For example, in the now famous experiments conducted at the University of Wisconsin-Madison, Harry Harlow conducted an experiment with Rhesus monkeys. He took infant monkeys and divided them into two groups and two subgroups. Group A was put in a room with a metallic mother figure (a fake mother monkey made of metal wiring); one subgroup with the mother holding a bottle, and the other with no food. Group B was put in a room cloth covered, warm mother figure; again, one subgroup where the mother had a bottle, and the other with no bottle. Over time, the development of the two groups diverged greatly. The group with the cloth monkey mother, whether she had food or not, developed normally. They were able to form positive social connections with other monkeys, were confident, but still would retreat to Mom when needed. The other group didn't do so well. They were nervous, anxious, didn't form social relationships, and avoided their moms. This study has been replicated and expanded with human infants (but in a humane setting).

Researchers have concluded there are three attachments styles: secure, anxious, and avoidant/hostile:

- The *secure attachment* style is what it sounds like. A child who has a secure attachment feels safe, has the ability to be curious, loves his caregivers, can connect with others and can retreat to their caregivers when needed.

- A child who has an *anxious attachment* doesn't move very far away from their primary caregiver. They are afraid of strange situations and new people. They feel safe when they are with their caregiver, and anxious when away. They don't feel safe to explore or to be curious, and they have trouble connecting with others.

- The last style, the *avoidant/hostile attachment* style, is characterized by a child who is indifferent whether their caregiver is near or not. These children don't explore, they don't make positive connections with others, and they can even be hostile to others and their caregiver. The sad part is that attachment styles extend into adulthood. Changing one's attachment style can happen, but it takes serious personal effort and counseling for healing to occur.

Batman clearly has an avoidant attachment style. We'll explore that more, and what he can do to heal. Furthermore, Bruce may very well be suffering from the effects of PTSD. Having covered what's wrong with Batman, in the next section I'll cover what I could do for Batman if he walked into my counseling office seeking services.

The Counseling

Like Spider-Man, Batman has experienced great loss in his life. I would walk Batman through the four tasks of grieving. Like Punisher, you could argue that Batman is suffering from PTSD. You could even make a stronger case for PTSD with Batman than The Punisher. Batman is driven like no other superhero. He constantly pushes himself beyond his limits. He's a man running from the ghosts that haunt his past. In The Punisher chapter, three interventions were mentioned for PTSD: talk therapy, medication, and support groups. Let's zoom in on the talk therapy option for a second. If I were to treat Batman using talk therapy, I would something exposure therapy to help him work through his PTSD.

Exposure therapy would consist of taking Batman to places that trigger the PTSD reaction. Exposure would begin in the mind. I would have Batman imagine the scene of his parents' death. As Batman is mentally going back that place, I would help him soothe his fear, anxiety and anger. Ways of accomplishing this are deep breathing, positive self-talk and accepting the loss (refer to the "relaxation skills" mentioned in the "Punisher" chapter). Once he has reached a level of control, I would raise the stakes. I would have him re-watch the news coverage of his parent's death. Again, Batman would use the skills to manage his feelings and reduce stress when the PTSD reaction occurs. Once he achieves mastery at that level, I would take him back to the physical site of his parents' death and walk through what happened. If the experience becomes overwhelming (it most likely will), Batman now has a set of skills to manage the overpowering feelings. Stress-reduction skills don't remove the pain; they allow Batman to face his parents' death and process the pain. Exposure therapy may seem harsh, but the alternative is someone never facing what happened, never processing their feelings and, therefore, never healing. They will always be running. Up to this point, Batman has been running because he can't accept the loss. Exposure therapy gives him a chance at healing.

In combination with the exposure therapy, I would also do Cognitive Behavioral Therapy (CBT). I would challenge Bruce Wayne's idea that he was responsible for his parents' death. This notion is evident in the *Final Crisis* storyline and, frankly, it's present whenever Batman's psychology is probed. He holds himself responsible for their deaths, and this is the reason he's afraid to get close to anyone. He's afraid they will be hurt, an inherent risk for anyone in proximity to Batman. It is also a self-protective measure, in that, if he is never close to someone, he can never be hurt by someone. Self-blame is an obstacle for Bruce in facing and accepting what happened to his parents that night.

The second focus of counseling is building healthy attachments with people. After the death of Bruce's parents, it's likely that he formed an avoidant attachment style. Like I said before, one's attachment style carries into adulthood. This is evidenced by the fact that Batman always works alone. About the only positive connection he has is to Alfred. But, I also did say your style can be modulated. Batman has had sidekicks named "Robin," four of them in fact.

The first was Dick Grayson. Grayson eventually moved on and became Nightwing. The second Robin was Jason Todd. He was murdered by the Joker.[8] After Todd came Tim Drake, the third Robin; then Stephanie Brown, the fourth. That's a lot of sidekicks for someone who avoids connection. So what gives? Batman always accepts his partners begrudgingly, but then realizes how necessary it is to have a companion. Deep down he knows he needs others; it's just uncomfortable for him. Two heads are better than one, right?

So, here are a few things I would work on with Batman:

- *Relinquish guilt* for things outside your control, i.e. death of parents, death of Jason Todd.

---

[8] In *A Death in the Family*, Joker captures Jason Todd and his mother. He beats Todd severely then blows the building up. Batman races to the building, but he's too late. He finds Todd dead.

- *Relinquish shame* for having emotional needs. Needs are not a sign of weakness. It is, in fact, a courageous thing to be vulnerable and honest with your friends and family about what you need.
- *Join a support group* of fellow sufferers. They can work with you on relational issues. Man is not an island; people were made to be in relationship with other people. It is a basic human need.
- *Accept yourself*—good, bad, warts and all. We've all made mistakes and no one is perfect. Perfection is an illusion. So, stop beating yourself up for not attaining something that is impossible.
- *Learn to be assertive* by expressing your needs. Having a need for connection, affection, community and love isn't a sign of weakness. You wouldn't think this about food, water or shelter. So why, then, would you think it about emotions? Emotional needs are just as essential as physical needs.
- *Develop healthy boundaries.* It's okay that you are uncomfortable with too much relational contact. It's safe to share that with those you love. Sharing your

boundaries creates respect and relational health.

I would walk through these things with Batman very slowly and patiently. It is exceedingly difficult to face wounds like Batman's. But it isn't impossible to heal. Maybe you can relate. It's okay to admit your hurts and wounds. It's okay to need other people. Our hurts and wounds almost have a life of their own. They will feed us lies so they can stay alive. Because, once you start the healing process, they have no place to live. Don't buy the lie. We encounter all our hurts in relationship, and we experience all our healing in relationship. Get out there and find a group you feel safe with. Reconnect with that old friend. Or, call that family member you need to bury the hatchet with. Trust me: you'll be glad you did.

Superman

"It's a bird... it's a plane... it's Superman!" The Man of Steel, son of Krypton, mild-mannered Clark Kent is the greatest of all Earth's superheroes, and he's not even from here (don't tell Donald Trump). Superman is the greatest superhero of Earth, of all time. Whoa. Those are fighting words! Of course, whoever holds the mantle of "greatest" is under hot debate. (I believe Batman actually has the most votes according to an online survey.) But, really? Except for Captain Marvel, who else can take on Superman? I guess we'll save that debate for another time.

Even though Superman may be the most powerful superhero—indestructibility, heat vision, cold breath, x-ray vision, super-hearing (but no super-smelling?), flight, super-strength, super-agility, incredible speed (ugh, this list is exhausting)—he also has some weaknesses. Depending on which Superman storyline you follow, either Superman is naturally super or he gets his super-ness from the Earth's sun. That means Superman is dependent upon light from our solar system's star. What does he do if he doesn't have access to the Sun's light? Furthermore, Superman is deathly allergic to Kryptonite (an understatement)! He also goes weak in the knees for a certain female reporter, Lois Lane. Oh yeah, and Superman dies at the hands of Doomsday. So yeah, he's got some weaknesses. We've established some powers and abilities, but what about Superman's psychology? What makes the Man of Steel tick?

Counseling Service for Superman

It is conceivable that Superman could struggle with anxiety—the anxiety of knowing everyone's problem and also being in a position to help. The movie *Man of Steel* illustrated this well. When Clark was a young man just discovering his powers, his super senses were overwhelming. Most people struggle with anxiety because they feel like the problems in their lives are outside of their control. Superman has the exact opposite problem. He has the power to help, but there's only one of him. The need of humanity is so overwhelming it could drive someone crazy. So, what is the Son of Krypton to do? Superman has responded throughout the comics in three ways.

- **Response #1:** In the face of humanity's overwhelming cry of need, Superman isolates as a way of avoiding anxiety.
- **Response #2:** Instead of avoiding people Superman alleviates anxiety by controlling everything around him.
- **Response #3:** Superman learns to cope with the anxiety by understanding his limitations, establishing healthy boundaries and doing self-care.

Isolation

As for the first response to anxiety, we see this played out the comic *Kingdom Come*. The Earth is in peril, but Superman is nowhere to be found. He's retreated to the JLA space station where he's living a life of solitude working on his simulated Kent farm. But the idyllic scene is rudely interrupted when Wonder Woman pleads with

Superman to save the Earth one more time. Superman resists the request at first, but is overcome by a sense of responsibility. When you're Superman, the life of a hermit is impossible (poor Superman).

The life of a hermit is also impossible for us lowly non-super human types. I've worked with many clients who have sworn off contact with other people. They tell me their plan for just going to school, or work and not talking to people. They do this for several reasons: hurt, anger, fear, social discomfort. But the solution of avoidance or isolation is irrational.

Community is an essential need. Just as you need food, water and shelter, you also need other people. Furthermore, avoidance of interpersonal problems keeps your personal development stalled. Community, family, friends, intimate partners hold a mirror to our souls. They point out aspects of ourselves that we would normally miss. In other words, they point out our blind spots. Having a blind spot pointed out provides an opportunity for growth. But this opportunity is never afforded if you always avoid people.

Control

In *Superman: Red Son*, the space craft that delivered Superman from Krypton to Earth was slightly disrupted. Instead of landing in Smallville, Kansas on the Kent Farm, Superman lands in the Ukraine on a collective farm. This small change dramatically changes Superman's story. Instead of fishing for "truth, justice and the American way," he becomes a champion of the Soviet Union. He eventually takes over the country. As he governs, in order to keep people safe, he has to keep increasing his level of control. Freedom takes a hit for the promotion of security, which eventually embitters the citizens of the Soviet Union against their leader. Control has a tendency of building resentment in others.

If you struggle with control, what can you do to change? First, the very best thing you can do is realize that you cannot change another person. Forcibly changing or controlling another person leads you down a path of disrespect, distrust and regret. The reason being, people are complicated. They are a mixture of past experiences, dreams, hopes, and fears. There is no formula for changing or controlling another human being. And those who thus try to change and control, are abusive.

What about trying to control things other than people? The same thinking applies. You can't control situations or events. When it comes to the economy, who gets elected, downsizing in your company, the weather, these things are simply out of your direct control. You can try your best to influence them in your favor, but at the end of the day, your control is limited.

So stop spending all your time on things outside your control and focus on what is inside your control. Two clinical terms help explain the difference between what is inside and outside your control. For things inside your control, the clinical term is *Internal Locus of Control*; for what is outside your control, the clinical term is *External Locus of Control*. Let's look at these two categories.

Internal Locus of Control

Internal Locus of Control is a fancy way of saying "where you locate the center of control in your life." The internal would be *inside of* you, the external would be *outside* of you. The things that you can directly influence or change are the things inside your locus of control. For example, you can directly control what you eat, when you go to bed, how much water you drink in a day, how you respond to co-workers, and how often you look at your smartphone. No one else can make you do these things; they are totally and completely done by your choosing. Psychologists suggest that instead of focusing on what is outside their control, people redirect their attention to what they *can* control. What is it within your direct sphere of influence that you can change?

External Locus of Control

The things you would put in this category are what you cannot or should not try to control. Like I said above, you can't control the shifts in the economy, the behavior of your co-workers, the attitudes of your spouse, or the weather. These things operate independently of you. Many people try to control what they cannot. This either makes them unhappy, mentally ill or a "control freak." Instead of trying to control what is outside your control, psychologists suggest that you radically accept them. Accept them for what they are and focus on what you can change within yourself and your life. This brings us to the next section: what if Superman tried to control everything?

Messiah Complex and Boundaries

If Superman developed a messiah-complex and eventually go insane with trying to fix everything. But is it Superman's job to fix all our problems? This isn't a question of capability. Obviously, Superman has the ability to fix many of the world's issues. It's more a question about if he *should*. Take caterpillars, for example. Caterpillars struggle to break free from their cocoon; the struggle is difficult to watch, and you may have the impulse to help the caterpillar out of its cocoon. But if you do this before it has had the chance to fight its way out, it will die. Why? It is the struggle that enables it to have the strength to supports its wings as a butterfly. If Superman continually bails humanity out from its self-created problems, will humanity ever learn? If humanity can't learn, can humanity grow? If humanity can't grow, then we will be dependent. I guess if Superman was concerned about job security, that's one route he could go, but I think he'd like to one day retire. And that can never happen if humanity is dependent upon him. Superman will have to learn boundaries. He will have to let humanity struggle.

Letting those you love struggle is difficult to do. I often see parents fight against the idea, but anyone can be guilty of it: spouses, co-workers, friends, dating couples. The problem with taking on another person's problems for them is that you remove their chance to learn and grow. You cut open their cocoon before they develop the strength to fly. Deep down, I think Superman knows this is true. Therefore, I would work with him on determining the line between helping and enabling dependence. How about you? Do you struggle with people-pleasing? With enabling another's dependence? I would challenge you to rethink your idea of "helping." The help you provide others may not be help at all.

Personal Limitations and Self-Care

You are a limited creature. Some consider this fact is a curse. We want to have unlimited time, energy, and resources so we can achieve all our ambitions in life. This is a fantasy. Regardless of how talented and hardworking you are, there is only so much you can do in a day. You have a limited supply of resources every day, therefore, you can't satisfy every demand, nor should you. Limitations force you to acknowledge your needs. It is physically, emotionally, financially, and mentally impossible for you to say yes to every request, demand or life challenge. At some point, you will need help.

Accepting your limitations will help learn to advocate for you own needs, ask for help when you need it, and be humble. These concepts fit nicely with the discussion in the previous section about boundaries. Learning to say no is a great boundary to have, although a difficult one to master. I've worked with many clients who struggle with this. They feel pressure to always have an answer, to always have the solution, and to always say yes. But no one can survive with that kind of pressure. You must have the courage and strength to enforce healthy boundaries. When you can do this, you have respectfully cared for yourself and for others. If Superman can acknowledge his limits, than you can too!

Wonder Woman

The Amazonian warrior princess Wonder Woman wields the Lasso of Truth, indestructible bracelets, and weaponized tiara. She is beautiful. She fights for justice, love and peace. Yes, princess Diana of Themyscira, aka Diana Prince, is a force to be reckoned with. The story of her creation is almost as interesting as the character's story itself. The psychologist William Moulton Marston, creator of the polygraph, was asked to be a consultant for the precursor company of DC. They were so impressed with Marston that they asked him to come up with his own comic book character. And so, Wonder Woman was born. But the most interesting part of Wonder Woman's creation was that Marston created her as female empowerment propaganda. He used the Greek myth of the Amazons, a society of strictly females, as his muse. Wonder Woman embodies the power and strength of her male counterparts while utilizing her feminine attributes as an asset. Marston designed Wonder Woman not to defeat her enemies with strength, but with love.

This was only the first iteration of Wonder Woman. The character was revamped after *Crisis on Infinite Earths*. [9] The revamped heroine had power conferred from the gods. She had "beauty from Aphrodite, strength from Demeter, wisdom from Athena, speed and flight from Hermes, Eyes of the Hunter and unity with beasts from Artemis and sisterhood with fire and the ability to discern the truth from Hestia." [10] She left her homeland, the Amazon, to live in the United States. Throughout her story she loses her powers, and

---

[9] *Crisis on Infinite Earths* was a seminal event in the DC universe. In short, it ended all the variant timelines and storylines, simplifying the DC universe down to one Earth, one universe, one storyline for all the characters, including Wonder Woman.

[10] Colluccio, Ali. "Top 5: Wonder Woman Reboots". iFanboy. *Retrieved April 10, 2012.*

goes back and forth between the U.S. and Amazon, all leading up to a critical point in her story. Wonder Woman was forced to kill an alternate-universe evil Superman. [11] Little did Wonder Woman know, her killing of evil Superman was broadcast to the whole world. Fast forward: Wonder Woman is thrust into an alternate timeline where she never existed and her memory is impaired. She fights to return Earth to its correct timeline, and for her own identity. Aside from the action and fantastical elements, Wonder Woman's story raises to our attention an uncomfortable aspect of everyday life, identity. Therefore, if Wonder Woman wandered into my office seeking help, this is what I would do.

Welcoming Wonder Woman to Counseling

Who are you when you don't remember who you are? How do you perceive yourself when people judge you based on one moment, one action? What causes you to accept or reject the statements other make about your identity? Good

---

[11] As a side note, unlike other superheroes and superheroines, Wonder Woman is comfortable with deadly force when deemed appropriate.

questions, right? Well, let's dive into the topic of identity.

Sadly, life is inherently unfair. We don't get the breaks we want or deserve. People treat us poorly. Opportunities are missed or taken away. And life rarely seems to work in our favor. But you must ask yourself this question, is life that way because it's designed for us to fail or because we give in too quickly when there's a struggle?

As in most things, the answer is usually somewhere in the middle. Yes, some things are outside our control. Such is life and there's nothing you can do about it. Tires go flat on the highway; family members get sick; the economy sometimes changes in your favor and sometimes not; your favorite NFL team loses their seat to the playoffs year after year. What are you are going to do? Such is life. But this axiom of reality does not extend to everything. There are things in your life that are attainable. You can achieve your goals if you put the work in. And these things aren't doomed from the get-go. They aren't out of our control.

It is your identity—what you want in life, who you believe you are, the content of your character, the strength of your resolve, integrity—that determines what your goals are. Furthermore, it is your identity that gives you the drive to achieve them.

So, let me ask you, who are you? Socrates, the Athenian philosopher of ancient Greece, thought this was the most important question you could ask yourself. He considered himself a gadfly because he would irritate or disrupt people's lives by forcing them, through questions, to look at unexamined areas of their life. Plato recorded Socrates' famous saying "The unexamined life is not worth living!" Through the process of examination, the listeners of Socrates' questions were "born" into the truth. In other words, Socrates assisted the birth of self-discovery, like a midwife. The power of Socrates' philosophy persists because many recognize knowledge of self has ultimate personal importance.

Let's go to the next step. To discover who you are, ask yourself—*What are my values? Whom do I look up to? What do I think is right and wrong? What am I willing to take from other people? What is important to me? What are my goals in life? How do I see myself? What do I want to accomplish with my life? What do I want my legacy to be? What kind of example do I want to set for my kids or the future generations?*

      Why are these questions important? These questions matter a lot because when someone challenges who you are, you don't have to accept what they say. Let's say your boss wants you to do something unethical to advance the interests of the company. What do you do? Allow your boss to have his way at the cost of your own ethics? At the future risk of you being caught and taking the blame? What do you do? This isn't a theoretical question or one for the philosophers; this is a question, a dilemma, a matter of identity that happens all the time. Who you are determines what you do. If you consider yourself a person of principle, of sound ethics, your boss's request would violate what you believe and threaten your integrity. And what you should do would be clear. If you were unsure, you could be persuaded to do something wrong and personally harmful. See where I'm going? Your identity gives you a roadmap on how to respond to dilemmas. When someone blocks you from attaining your goals because of their selfishness, you know that they need to be challenged. Too often, we allow others to get away with murder because we have no clue of who we are.

Accepting or Rejecting Another's Perception

Wonder Woman is faced with the option of either accepting the story being sold to her by others—that she's a murderer—or she can reject that story. To put the killing of the evil Superman in context, Wonder Woman killed Maxwell Lord. Maxwell Lord was from an alternate universe. He was able to control the Superman of his universe. He altered Superman's perception so that he would view Wonder Woman as his arch-enemy, Doomsday. In a series of events, Superman was about to kill Batman. Wonder Woman slit Superman's throat with her tiara and forced Lord to tell her how to end the mind control with her Lasso of Truth. Lord admitted there was no way to end the control unless he was killed. Wonder Woman then snapped the neck of Lord, saving Batman and herself from Superman's violent, mind-controlled attacks. When you put Wonder Woman's actions in context, you can see why she did what she did. But, only the killing was recorded and broadcast and, therefore, the world believed she was a killer. To make matters worse, Wonder Woman's memory was impaired. So put yourself in her shoes for a minute. You don't remember all the details from your past, and everyone is judging and labeling you as a murderer. What do you choose to believe?

Like Wonder Woman, I'm sure people have unfairly judged you. They hear rumors, have a bad first impression, or run into you on a bad day. Based on that one piece of information they form their opinion of you. Right or wrong, that opinion then creates a box that you cannot escape from. That opinion, based on limited information and experience, influences their interpretation of all that you do going forward. So, what do you do? Do you buy their interpretation, internalizing it as your identity? Or, do you challenge it?

You will have struggles and battles in your life, and that much goes without saying. But the question that will determine if you fight, if you find your voice and use it, if you stand up for your dream is, *Do you know who you are*?

Joker

Homicidal maniac, nihilist, domestic terrorist, super-villain, criminal mastermind— whatever you want to call him, the Joker is one bad dude. The Joker may very well be one of the greatest super-villains of all time. Ironic, since Joker's counterpart, Batman, is arguably the greatest superhero of all time. But not much is known about where Joker comes from. There are many possibilities. The most likely of these, simply because it offers the best juxtaposition with Batman, is the story of Joker falling into a vat of acid while fleeing from Batman. The acid discolored his skin, turned his hair green, and his lips bright red. After seeing his appearance, Joker went insane.

The parallels and divergences between him and Batman are uncanny. Batman experienced tragedy early on, and dedicated his life to goodness. Joker experienced tragedy early on, and dedicated his life to evil. They were made for each other. Neither possesses super-abilities. Both fell in love with women who were at one time adversaries. Batman fell in love with Selina Kyle, a small-time thief who burgled from Bruce Wayne. Joker fell in love with Harley Quinn, his psychiatrist at Arkham Asylum. They are a sort of *yin* and *yang*, two opposites who are locked in eternal battle.

But Joker isn't just Batman's nemesis, forcing us to ask the question, who really is the Joker? Batman, Gotham's police department, the Arkham Asylum psychiatry staff, even Joker's associates—they all think he's *crazy*. They say he's a psychotic killer. These allegations aren't far off from the truth. Joker has personally killed dozens of people and even derailed a train. Yet, he wasn't always that way. Originally, he was a fledgling comedian who struggled to support his pregnant wife.[12] In order to make ends meet,

---

[12] As told in *Batman*: *The Killing Joke* which is considered the definitive Joker origin story.

Joker joins up with a criminal to rob a chemical plant that Joker used to work for. The criminals force Joker to assume the identity of Red Hood. On the day they were going to execute their plan, Joker learns that his pregnant wife died, yet Joker went through the robbery despite his grief. Batman interferes with Red Hood's nefarious plan, accidentally causing him to fall into a vat of acid. Red Hood, seeing his garish appearance that resembles a clown, assumes a new identity, the Joker.

At first, the Joker was a prankster, a foil for the dynamic duo. As the story evolved, the Joker was sent to Arkham Asylum where he was deemed legally insane. In a horrifying chain of events,[13] Joker beats Jason Todd (Batman's second Robin) severely with a crowbar and then blows him and his mother up. Batman arrives at the scene too late. He finds his young partner, dead. This takes the Joker from a low-level, insane prankster to the killer of a superhero.

---

[13] Explained in *A Death in the Family.*

Psychology for the Psychopath

The Joker, a fascinating character in his own right, offers insights into human nature. In *Batman: The Killing Joke*, Joker fatally wounds Barbara Gordon, daughter of Commissioner Gordon, and takes nude photos of her bleeding out. He tortures the captured Commissioner Gordon by stripping him naked, bound and gagging, and forcing him to look at the photos. Joker states that he wants to prove that it only takes one bad day to turn a sane man into a psychopath. Later on, Joker goes one step further and murders Commissioner Gordon's wife, Sarah. This is revealing of Joker's character and worldview, but it also provides a mirror for humanity. Is it true that a relatively good person can be corrupted after one event? Is the dividing line between good and evil so thin? Does it really only take one bad day to turn a sane man insane? Joker's point is that humanity possesses a dark side. Those who appear good, respectable, and outwardly virtuous are deluding themselves, or giving a false impression. In his mind, goodness is the illusion; evil is humanity's real condition.

Batman, on the other end of the spectrum, is the paragon of incorruptibility; regardless of what happens, Batman's integrity remains. In other words, circumstances won't compromise his commitment to his ethics. He is the antithesis to Joker. Yet, even though Joker hates Batman, many times Joker reveals that he would be incomplete without him. At one point, Joker steals the ability to alter the universe, remaking it to fit his vision. He tortures Batman daily. Intending to destroy the universe, the only thing that holds him back is his reluctance to kill Batman. This small hesitation gives Superman the opportunity to stop Joker and restore the universe.[14]

More on Personality Disorders

I was tempted to lump Joker into the same camp as Thanos. I thought Joker was a nihilist, too. Upon reflection, I don't think that's true. I think Joker is more an anarchist than a nihilist. In *The Dark Knight Rises* movie, directed by Christopher Nolan, Alfred compares the Joker to a criminal he was hunting in Bolivia. Bruce and Alfred go back and forth, Alfred sharing the story as an analogy for understanding the Joker. Alfred concludes his story with, "Some men just want to watch the

---

[14] This story is from *Emperor Joker*.

world burn." I would argue that the Joker is more self-destructive than Thanos, but he's not a nihilist. Joker doesn't want to see everything destroyed. On the contrary, he would rather see the institutions and structures of society destroyed so that humanity's mask of morality can be removed. He is an anarchist in the truest sense of the word.

Therefore, I think it's likely that the Joker suffers from *Antisocial Personality Disorder* (APD). Often I hear people misuse the term antisocial for someone who is introverted. Antisocial doesn't mean you're against being social. It means you're against society. In fact, I have worked with clients with this diagnosis whom I found very socially adept. APD has nothing to do with someone's ability to make friends. It's more about how someone with APD disregards the rights, entitlements, feelings, thoughts, and needs of others. Given the opportunity to benefit oneself and screw someone else over, a person with this disorder wouldn't think twice. They'd immediately go with the option that benefits themselves without any regard for the other person. The impact of their actions on others means little to them. Someone diagnosed with APD would feel no remorse or regret for actions that harmed another. Furthermore, someone with APD could be very charming, violent, abusive, egotistical, and impulsive. He lacks regard for right and wrong, enjoys risk-taking, is a chronic liar and has issues with the legal system. Hmm... who does that sound like to you? Bingo! Joker fits the profile perfectly.

Psychotic Disorder

The Joker is often described as "psychotic" by filmmakers. Comic book and game writers often use the term *psychotic* to describe Joker with greater clarity. But does Joker actually meet the clinical and diagnostic criteria? *Psychotic Disorder* (PD) is primarily defined as a break with reality. Their thoughts and perceptions are abnormal. Psychotic people perceive things (visual and auditory) that are not there (hallucinations), see attacks where there are none (paranoia), or believe things that aren't true (delusions). Schizophrenia is a Psychotic Disorder and Bipolar Disorder can have PD features. Drugs and alcohol, brain tumors, strokes and brain infections can also cause PD. Knowing this, could I diagnose the Joker with PD?

Honestly, no. He perceives threats from his enemies; that's not abnormal. He's not hallucinating Batman, Superman, or Wonder Woman; they're real (in the fictional sense). So that rules out hallucination. Batman has done harm to Joker and he does want to apprehend him. The threat to Joker is real: that's not paranoia.

Finally, I don't see any evidence of delusions. Joker is correct in his observation that mankind has a dark side. His primary goal is to destroy the structures and institutions of society, thus creating anarchy. Joker is making an assumption that when those structures are gone, humanity will be revealed for the degenerate animal it is. This isn't delusional. In fact, Joker sits comfortably in the same camp of philosophers such a Thomas Hobbes, Friedrich Nietzsche, and Arthur Schopenhauer.

Joker wants to destroy the social order and expose, what he believes to be, the true nature humanity as evil through acts of violence, murder, terrorism, and anarchy. That's not delusional, that's just evil. Therefore, I'd be hard pressed to diagnose Joker with PD. I think it's more likely that Joker suffers from a personality disorder. I think he is called "psychotic" for two reasons. First, writers use that term for dramatic effect. Second, there is cultural confusion about psychoses represented by comic book writers.

Allow me to get on my mental health soapbox for a moment. Our culture is depressingly illiterate when it comes to the mental health field. We use terms like "crazy," "psycho," "lunatic," and "nuts" to describe people with mental health issues. But the reality is, at some point in your life, or the life of someone close to you, you or they will struggle with a mental health disorder. Also, a person with a mental health diagnosis is no more dangerous than any other person. The perception that people with mental illnesses are dangerous, violent and hostile is simply untrue. The saddest part is that cultural misperceptions create a negative stigma. Stigma has a number of harmful effects. Stigma keeps those suffering with mental illness at arm's length from others. They remain on the fringe, since stigma blocks them from integrating with society, which in turn keeps them from getting the help, support and services they need. This divide inhibits understanding between those who suffer from mental illness and those who don't. This makes it taboo to admit a problem and seek help. And this should not be. I challenge you to be an agent of change. Share your story of struggling with mental health issues, or go public with your support of someone who does. Mental illness isn't abnormal or abhorrent. It's normal. I'm stepping off my soapbox now. Phew!

Help for a Heckler

So, if the Joker waltzed into my office, how would I counsel him? Like I said with Thanos, personality disorders are frankly hard to "cure." I would engage Joker in psychotherapy to confront some of his evil patterns of thinking. He sees no problem in hurting others for his personal gain, but how would he feel if someone did that to him? A lack of empathy is one symptom of APD. Therefore, the aim of counseling would be to raise Joker's level of empathy for others. Joker simply doesn't think about how his actions affect another person. For some, empathy may not come naturally. But that's not an excuse to live life without empathy. Empathy can be learned as a skill. Now, that may sound easy enough, but when it comes to personality disorders, what I just described would be a lot of work. We're talking years of work, with little progress. Like I said in the Thanos chapter, personality disorders are native to the person. They are ingrained into who they are. You are trying to change a dysfunctional piece of someone's identity, which is very hard and long work, but not impossible. Here's my empathy boot camp for Joker:

- **Become a student of people**. Make observations of what people say, how they say it, and how people respond.
- **Become Emotionally Intelligent**. Emotion is at the core of humanity. To truly understand the experience of another human being, you must understand how they feel. This requires empathy, the ability to put yourself in someone else's shoes.
- **Become an Active Listener**. Empathy can only be achieved through understanding. And you can't understand another person unless you are willing to listen to them. That means laying down your own agenda and listening to, not just

hearing, what the other person is experiencing, feeling and thinking.

- **Become aware of yourself.** Self-understanding can be a key for understanding others. Become attuned to your own feelings and responses to others. Then become attuned to how others respond to you.

- **Become a person of respect.** Observation, listening, and understanding are built on the foundation of respect. If you value and consider yourself a person of dignity, you must give that same consideration to others.

Another area I would work on is changing the environment that Joker lives in. That means engaging family, friends, and associates in Joker's process of change. Change is impossible without the support from one's community. Therefore, Joker's community needs psycho-education on APD. They need specific coping skills to use when dealing with Joker. Secondly, I would teach them skills on how to gently but firmly confront Joker's APD. One voice working for change may not be enough. But, if Joker's community is unified, over time he will eventually listen. Personality change is a hard road travel and must be traveled with others, but the end result is worth the work.

Silver Surfer

Norrin Radd, a young astronomer from the planet Zenn-La, paid the ultimate price to save his home. Given the option of destruction or a life of slavery, Radd chose to spare his world and became the Silver Surfer, herald of Galactus. But slavery came with a few perks. Norrin Radd was imbued with Galactus' Power Cosmic and given a spacecraft in the shape of a surfboard that could travel faster than the speed of light. Silver Surfer was tasked with the mission to find suitable planets for Galactus to consume. Surfer tried his best to find uninhabited planets. Over time, planets were harder and harder to find. It also became increasingly difficult to maintain his individuality and memory. The longer Norrin Radd was the Silver

Surfer, less of himself remained. He was becoming a zombie-like servant of Galactus.

Surfer was desperate when he came to Earth. While scouting the new planet, Silver Surfer met the Fantastic Four. The new friends helped Silver Surfer rediscover the man within, forcing a moral crisis that Surfer had long been avoiding. Surfer rebelled against Galactus and saved Earth, but as a consequence, he was exiled to our planet. Surfer's story alone would make him a compelling character; however, it is his ability to think deeply about his situation that makes him unique. One could even call him the philosopher-superhero.

The History of the Herald

Norrin Radd was born and raised on Zenn-La, as you know. What you may not know is that Zenn-La was a highly advanced planet. It was utopia. Zenn-La culture advanced to the point of eradicating poverty, hunger, homelessness, disease, war and crime. It was a perfect society. Since there were no problems to fix, the citizens of Zenn-La focused strictly on maximizing pleasure. Zenn-La put the Greek hedonists to shame. Yet the hedonistic lifestyle didn't satisfy everyone.

Radd's parents, Elmar and Jartran, were unique. They didn't want to lives of aimless hedonism. They were intellectually, philosophically driven. They loved and pursued knowledge. Sadly, both eventually committed suicide, leaving behind two sons, Norrin and Fennan. Norrin followed in his parents' footsteps. He, compelled by a sense of morality rather than pleasure, sacrificed his own freedom to save his planet and become Galactus' slave. Thankfully for Surfer, after his rebellion and exile to Earth, he eventually won his freedom to wander the universe. Surfer was glad to leave Earth since he lost his faith in humanity after encountering the dark side of humanity. Yet his wanderings proved a disappointment as well. Surfer explores the universe only to find melancholy.

Help for the Herald

Imagine Silver Surfer taking a break from his exploration and reflection on the universe to stop by my office for a session. As a counselor, I wouldn't waste much time. After hearing his story, I am obligated to address certain issues such as suicidality with urgency. Given that both of Silver Surfer's parents committed suicide, there may be a genetic trait of suicidality that runs in the family. That is a risk factor for Silver Surfer which would prompt me to ask him if he's ever considered killing or harming himself. Family history alone doesn't warrant concern. However, when you take into account other biographical events such as the loss of his freedom, slavery to Galactus, the compulsion to identify planets for destruction, the torture of mind control, and his exile on planet Earth, such traumatic events are risk factors. Moreover, it is a risk factor that he's prone to melancholy when wandering the universe. These two sets of risk factors—the environmental in combination with the genetic—could activate a latent suicidal trait. That would cause me concern.

Unfortunately, suicide is a serious problem in the United States. Little is understood about the nature of suicide. Often, family and friends of those who commit suicide are at a loss as to why their loved one killed themselves. The general population is largely uninformed about suicide, therefore, it is vital for the sake of your neighbors, family members, friends and co-workers that you learn as much as you can. Knowledge is power, and knowledge about mental health and suicide could help you to save another's life, or your own. The National Alliance on Mental Illness (NAMI) has put out a very helpful fact sheet about suicide. [15] All facts and figures below are from this document. According to the sheet, about 30,000 people commit suicide in America every year. 1 million Americans engage psychiatric services for suicidal thoughts, behaviors and attempts, making it the most common psychiatric emergency.

NAMI has identified risk factors that could lead to suicide:

- The single biggest risk factor for suicide is a history of suicidal behaviors and attempts.
- Over 90 percent of people who die by suicide have been diagnosed with mental illness.
- Some of the mental illnesses most commonly associated with suicide include depression, bipolar disorder,

---

[15] National Alliance of Mental Illness:
http://www2.nami.org/factsheets/suicide_factsheet.pdf.
Retrieval: January, 3rd, 2016.

schizophrenia, personality disorders (including borderline personality disorder), anxiety disorders (including post-traumatic stress disorder and panic attacks) and eating disorders (including bulimia nervosa and anorexia nervosa).

- Substance abuse and addiction are associated with an increased risk of suicide.

- More than one in three people who die from suicide are intoxicated, most commonly with alcohol or opiates (e.g. Heroin, Percocet [oxycodone]).

- The majority of completed suicides in America involve firearms and access to firearms is associated with a significantly increased risk of suicide.

- Older age is associated with increased risk of suicide.

- While women are more likely to attempt suicide, men are four times more likely to die by suicide.

- People of all races and ethnicities are at risk for suicide.

- People who feel socially isolated (e.g. divorced, widowed) are at increased risk of suicide compared to people who have responsibility for family members (e.g. people who are married or people with children)

- While scientists have not discovered one specific gene that causes suicide, it is known that people with a family history of suicide are at increased risk.

- People with a history of trauma (e.g. childhood abuse or combat experience) are at increased risk of suicide.

- Involvement in community or religious organizations may decrease the risk of suicide.

The two recommended treatments for someone dealing with suicidality are Cognitive Behavioral Therapy (CBT) and/or Dialectical Behavioral Therapy (DBT). In brief, I will explain each model below:

- **CBT**- In this model, thinking is the focus. Thoughts affect behavior, and behavior affects how a person feels and responds to others. If someone has a negative perspective of themselves, others, or the world in general, it could drive them to suicide. In order to help Surfer, I would challenge these negative thoughts, beliefs and perceptions, testing them against reality. No one is really all bad, a complete failure, unlovable, against whom the whole world is conspiring. When these beliefs are challenged, reality bears a different story. It's more likely that Surfer is a mix of good and bad, having some successes and failures, loved and hated by some, with the world providing open and closed doors. Testing thinking against reality (reality-testing) counteracts negativity that hijacks the brain.

- **DBT**- Whereas CBT focuses on thinking, DBT focuses on emotions. To manage emotional swings, DBT provides a framework and a set of skills called "emotional regulation skills." The first skill is called *Radical Acceptance*: this is a stance where someone fully and completely accepts whatever is outside their control. The second skill is *Self-Soothing*: this involves doing something to soothe each of your five senses (taste, touch, smell, hearing and sight). Doing something that feels good for the senses can ease emotional pain. The third skill is

Positive Self-Talk. This skill is twofold: recognizing negative self-talk and replacing it with positive self-talk. So, what is self-talk? The most influential person you will ever meet is looking at you in the mirror. What we tell ourselves—positive or negative, true or false, cruel or compassionate—directly impacts how we feel, think and respond. Negativity tinges your perspective, and that leads to more negativity. The good news? The same works for positivity: positivity leads to more positivity.

Like I said before, I would start off by asking Surfer if he's considering killing or harming himself. Depending on the answer, I would then ask if he's thought about it recently and if he has a history of suicide attempts. We know that Surfer has never made an attempt, but he's certainly contemplated not living: in clinical terms, this is called *Suicidal Ideation.* If he is considering suicide, I would create a no-harm contract with Surfer. This is no guarantee that a person won't kill themselves, but a contract will give Surfer and myself a plan in case of a crisis. In the agreement, Surfer would commit to call me, a friend, a crisis hotline or the police when he is in crisis. He would also commit to going to a hospital if he felt like harming or killing himself.

Medication can sometimes pose a risk if someone is suicidal. Either the person stops taking their mediation putting them at further risk for harming themselves. Or, a prescription for needed medication will run out if the client doesn't consistently see their psychiatrist. There is also the possibility someone uses the medication to commit suicide. Therefore, I would make an agreement with Surfer to either, take his medication regular, see a psychiatrist if he has run out, or if he doesn't have any meds, to go see a psychiatrist for evaluation and prescription. And, if he feels like he might use the meds to commit suicide, he could entrust his medication to a trusted friend or family member who could hold onto them for safekeeping. Finally, I would him to commit to removing all weapons, illicit drugs or any means of killing himself from his home. Again, the no-harm agreement isn't a fail-safe, but it does help. It provides Surfer with a plan on how to get help when he needs it.

Once our contract is worked out, we would come up with some DBT emotional regulation skills that he likes and would actually use in a crisis. This will soothe the emotional pain and allow him to think and decide to either help himself or reach out for help during a wave of intense feelings. When he's soothed the emotional pain to a manageable point, he can then use some CBT skills to evaluate the veracity of his negative thinking and mood.

Negativity is a like a sickness. It distorts what's true for what isn't. If Surfer can use the CBT skills to challenge his negative thinking with what he knows to be true, he can begin to pull himself out of the toxic suicidal state. He may need extra help at first, but the end goal would be for him to help himself when at risk.

If you, or someone you know, is struggling with suicide thoughts, behaviors or attempts, don't let yourself or them suffer in silence. Seek help! Tell a friend, family member, pastor or therapist what is going on. If no one is available, there are national organizations with crisis and help lines. You can call the Suicide Prevention Lifeline (1-800-273-8255) or visit www.suicidepreventionlifeline.org. There are many other organizations that you can reach out to like IMAlive (www.hopeline.com) or the American Foundation for Suicide Prevention (www.afsp.com). The resources and help are out there; all you need to do is to ask. Be a superhero and save your life, or the life of a friend, co-worker, or family member.

Stephen Strange

Doctor Strange, sorcerer supreme, master of black magic, former gifted neurosurgeon brings the "wiz" to "wizard." Sorry, that was corny, but I couldn't help myself. Stephen Strange, world-renowned surgeon, lost the use of his hands in a tragic car accident. Seeking salvation, he traverses the Himalayas to seek out a spiritual master. Learning the mystical arts, Stephen Strange transforms into Doctor Strange, one of the most powerful sorcerers on the planet. He possesses many tools in his arsenal, including the Cloak of Levitation, Eye of Agamotto, and the Book of Vishanti. With these powerful tools, Doctor Strange defends this reality from inter-dimensional beings seeking power, dominion and control over Earth.

Okay, that was the flashy highlight reel; let's get into some more detail. Stephen was born in 1930 to Eugene and Beverly Strange. When Stephen was 8, he was attacked by demons under the control of Karl Mordo. Stephen was rescued by the Ancient One, Earth's sorcerer supreme at the time. Stephen had two siblings, Donna and Victor. He was the oldest. When he was 11, young Stephen saved his sister's life. This event was formative. Having saved his sister's life, Stephen wanted to save others. Therefore, he pursued a medical degree.

Strange entered pre-med. And everything in Strange's life seemed to look up, but he would soon face a rash of losses that would test him beyond what he could imagine. On a family vacation, Donna suffered a debilitating cramp while swimming and drown. Stephen was the one to find her body. He felt personally responsible for her death. Despite the devastating loss, Stephen progressed through medical school, residency and practice, at an accelerated pace. Strange was extremely gifted and talented. This made him arrogant. Then, his mother Beverly died.

Stephen went into medicine save the lives of others, but the deaths of his sister and mother challenged his idealistic vision. Stephen continued in medicine, but he did so with a cold heart. He didn't want to get hurt again; consequently, he detached himself from the meaning of his job and only worked for the money and fame it brought him. Soon enough, money and recognition were all he cared about. Then his father grew ill. Afraid to face more grief, Stephen avoided seeing his dad. Victor, Stephen's younger brother, came to see his brother and demanded to know why he was avoiding their father. They had a disagreement. Victor rushed out of Stephen's apartment in anger and disappointment, but not watching where he was going. He walked into the path of an oncoming car. Stephen found Victor was near death, so he placed his brother's body in cold storage. He did this hoping that one-day medical technology would advance to the point where his brother could be saved.

Years later, Strange would encounter another tragedy involving a car. Strange was involved in a tragic car accident that damaged the nerves in his hands. He would never perform surgery again. Not able to accept the loss of functioning hands, Stephen expended every penny he had to find a remedy, but nothing worked. He was desperate and willing to try anything. He hears of an eastern healer, the Ancient One, who may be able to help him. He throws caution to the wind, traversing the Himalayas in search of this eastern master. Upon arriving at the master's palace, the Ancient One refuses to cure Strange's hands. Yet, he does allow him to stay.

Mordo, the Ancient One's apprentice, conspires against his master. Strange learns of the conspiracy and seeks to thwart Mordo. The plan fails and Mordo escapes. Out of anger towards Mordo, a growing sense of allegiance to the Ancient One, and intrigue with magical forces, Strange vows to learn the mystical arts and fight on the side of good. He becomes a master of magic and the mystical arts, eventually becoming the sorcerer supreme, defender of Earth.

Strange Reflections

Strange's story, aside from entertaining us, communicates a deep truth: money can't make you happy. Before the car accident, Stephen was arrogant, materialistic, and indifferent to others. He was all about himself. But the Doctor's story wasn't meant to end there; his life was destined for a greater purpose. Through a reversal of the "rags to riches" story, Stephen has it all, then loses everything. Yet, *loss* was his salvation.

Even though Stephen had every material need met, his spiritual needs went ignored. The damage to the nerves in his hands served as a wakeup call. He could no longer fill his life with material distractions. He had to face his true self. And what he saw, he didn't like. Coming in contact with the supernatural reality opened his eyes and as a result, he was morally and spiritually transformed.

For many years, the significance of spirituality has been ignored by the medical and mental health fields. However, the psychological and physical benefits of spirituality are now being researched and integrated into healthcare.

Here are the top five characteristics of spiritual people:[16]

- **Spiritual people are gracious.** Psychology has demonstrated that expressing gratitude is associated with many positive emotions, such as optimism, generosity with time and resources, and overall vitality. Spirituality encourages people to be positive, which may be expressed in many of these life practices.

- **Spiritual people are compassionate.** Compassion toward others is one the strongest correlates with living a spiritual life. A variety of positive or pro-social emotions have strong links with spiritualism, including the ability to feel good about the little things in life, and to look at the world through empathetic eyes.

---

[16] Psychology Today: https://www.psychologytoday.com/blog/cant-buy-happiness/201302/why-be-spiritual-five-benefits-spirituality. Retrieval: January, 15, 2016.

- **Spiritual people flourish.** Spirituality is linked to many important aspects of human functioning--spiritual people are optimistic, and have positive relationships, high self-esteem, meaning and purpose in life.

- **Spiritual people self-actualize.** Spiritual individuals strive toward a better life and consider personal growth and fulfillment as a central goal. Spirituality is considered a path toward self-actualization, because it requires people to focus on their internal values and work on becoming a better individual.

- **Spiritual people take time to savor life experiences.** Individuals who value spirituality take the time to reflect on their daily activities and ultimately build lasting memories of their experiences. Because spiritual people are more conscious of small, daily activities, they experience positive emotions associated with the smaller pleasures in life.

So, how did Stephen Strange stack up against these five characteristics of spiritual people? He was not gracious, but selfish. He was not compassionate, he was greedy. He was not flourishing, but floundering, moving forward without direction or purpose. He was not self-actualizing: instead, his personal growth was stalled. And he wasn't savoring life: he was trying to fill a vacuum in his life with wealth, fame and prestige. Yet, when Strange had a spiritual awakening, his "after" picture looked a lot better. He was kinder, considerate, cared for the plight and suffering of others. He dedicated his life to fighting on the side of good and enjoyed a community of friends—the Avengers, Fantastic Four, X-Men, other sorcerers across the globe, and Wong, his best friend. I don't know about you, but that's a completely different person to me. That's an entirely better quality of life. That's a transformed life.

When reading the story of Stephen Strange, do you find yourself wishing you could have a similar transformation? Is your life lacking in a way that you can't describe, as if something vital is missing, but you're not sure what it is? Have you focused so much of your attention on medical, psychological, monetary or pharmacological problems that you've neglected your spiritual needs? Your relationships, physical health, career satisfaction impact your mental health, but so does your spiritual life. When was the last time you honestly evaluated your spiritual life?

Let me get at this another way. Do you feel a sense of awe in your life? Do you feel a sense of purpose when you wake up? When you make important decisions, what guides you? Is there meaning to your life? Does your story fit into a larger story, a grand narrative? Are you connected to other people? Do you have a community that supports you? Do you feel compassion and are lead to serve others? What rejuvenates, inspires, convicts and encourages you? If you're not sure on some or most of these questions, you have a spiritual deficit in your life. Even if you don't like the religious aspect of spirituality, look into it at least for the psychological and physical benefits. If you are interested in developing your spiritual life here are some straightforward and practical ideas practiced by mentally healthy people:

- **Join a Faith Community**- Find a group that regularly meets for the purpose of connecting and supporting each other. A group that loves each other connects with a story bigger than their own and wants to do good. Connecting with a group like this is an amazing boost to physical and mental health.

- **Pray Every Day**- This should not be intimidating, although many are by prayer. Just talk to the divine presence in your life. Share your struggles, victories and needs. It's that simple.

- **Read Scripture**- Find a scripture that inspires, convicts, strengthens and encourages you. Read it on a consistent basis. This doesn't have to be a major commitment. 10-15 minutes is all you need and if you want to read more, then go for it!

- **Live Life with a Purpose**- Your life is about more than just you. Your story fits into a larger narrative. Align your words, actions and thoughts with that purpose. It will give you a sense of meaning and intention as you go through your day.

- **Help Others**- There is nothing more powerful than helping another person. People have attested that when going to out to bless another, they, in turn, are blessed. Helping another person can be "big" or "small," it doesn't matter. Doing good is always good.

- **Count your Blessings**- Develop an attitude of gratitude. Many social science studies have supported this notion. When you mentally review the things you are grateful for, your mood improves. Try keeping a journal to record what you are grateful for.

- **It is Better to Give**- It is true: it is better to give than receive. Giving to another person, cause, organization or charity bestows you with a sense of purpose. It broadens your perspectives. You become aware of lives, stories and needs outside of yourself. Always being self-focused can make corrode your mental health. Altruism is a mental health booster. Instead of buying that thing you don't really need, give money, food or your time to someone who could use it.

- **Notice Beauty**- Life is full of beautiful things, yet we tend to only notice the negative. Fight that tendency, because you are missing the most enriching aspects of life. Go to an art museum, take a hike, listen to your favorite piece of music, find and tell someone the funniest joke you've ever heard. These may seem like inconsequential things when faced with all the world's problems, but the beautiful side of life is paramount. It fills us with a sense of awe and humility. And *that* has inestimable value.

If you're spiritually out of shape, it may be hard to get into the rhythm. Millions and millions of people every day derive strength, encouragement, value, meaning and purpose from their spiritual life, and you can, too. Stephen Strange's story, although fictional, is nonetheless true. His story expresses a universal truth. People are spiritual beings. You wouldn't ignore your need for food, shelter, or community, so why would you ignore your spiritual needs. For some, it may take a catastrophic event, as in the case of Stephen Strange. Yet, it doesn't have to be that way. You can live a spiritually transformed life now.

Iron Man

Tony Stark, son of Howard Stark and heir of Stark Industries, MIT graduate, playboy, engineering genius and—did I fail to mention?— he's also Iron Man. Like Batman, The Punisher, and the Joker, Iron Man has no superpowers. He is a typical human being with exceptional intelligence. And it is his intelligence that enables him to be one of the strongest superheroes out there.

True to form, Iron Man's life has been touched by tragedy. When Tony was 21 his parents were killed in car accident orchestrated by ROXXON, Stark Industries rival. Tony inherited Stark Enterprises, but business wasn't his thing. He quickly appointed Pepper Potts to take over the day-to-day. Tony had his mind on other things, like building advanced weapon technology, which was the reason he attended a weapon field test at one of his international testing sites. After his arrival, Stark was attacked terrorists led by Wong Chu. During the attack a land mine exploded near Tony, lodging shrapnel in his heart. Held captive under threat of death, Tony, was forced to make Wong Chu a weapon. Wong Chu also kidnapped Professor Ho Yinsen, world famous physicist. Yinsen and Stark secretly set to work on creating a magnetic field generator. This device would prevent the shrapnel in Tony's heart from killing him. They built the field generator and a battle suit to go around it, and thus, Iron Man was born. Sadly, the creation of Iron Man came at a cost, the death of Professor Yinsen. Tony Stark, using his Iron Man suit, made the terrorists pay by breaking free and destroying their compound.

Tony returned home to his fiancée, Joanna Nivena, but there was trouble in paradise. In order to survive, Tony had to wear his armor's chest plate all the time in order to keep the shrapnel from advancing into his heart. He kept his injury and the suit secret, even from his fiancée. This was pure anguish for Tony. Living under constant threat of death, dependent upon a chest to keep him alive, was tremendous pressure. In order to cope with the anxiety, he started drinking heavily and even became suicidal. Things only got worse from there. Joanna, realizing Tony would never be the stable family man she wanted, broke the engagement off and left him. Tony bounced back, in a manner of speaking, by repurposing his chest plate and suit to serve a larger goal: he became the superhero Iron Man. Tony also founded and funded the Avengers. Additionally, he joined several other superhero organizations, such as the Fantastic Four, the Inhumans, X-Men, and the Illuminati.

Another key event happened in Tony's life. After witnessing the destructive power of weapons, Tony vowed to end munitions productions, renamed his company as Stark International, and put all his time and his company's resources into electronics and computer engineering. Unfortunately, the stress of competition with Justin Hammer, ROXXON's CEO, and the constant needs of S.H.I.E.L.D. [17] intensified Tony's alcoholism. Knowing this weakness, a competitor-turned-enemy, Obadiah

---

[17] S.H.I.E.L.D. is a covert government agency run by Nick Fury.

Stane, waged psychological, financial and physical warfare with Stark. In every way, Stane tried to exacerbate Tony's drinking. His tactics were effective. Tony drank to the point he lost control of his company. He was pushed out of his own company, which was then taken over by Stane. The once-playboy billionaire was homeless, penniless and perpetually drunk. Happily, Tony's story doesn't end there. As a matter of happenstance, Tony came upon a woman giving birth. He assisted in the delivery. This got Tony thinking about life and death, meaning and purpose. Soon after, he joined an Alcoholics Anonymous group and started down the path of recovery. Moving in with the West Coast Avengers, he resumed his role as Iron Man in battle with Stane, ultimately bringing him down.

Insight for Iron Man

If Tony pulled up in a Lamborghini and walked into my office, what would I do with him? In order to help Tony, it's necessary to take a deeper look into alcohol addiction. The point at which your drinking becomes a clinically diagnosable problem is when you are no longer able to perform your responsibilities, such as work, school, or parenting. Or when you drink in situations that are dangerous, like while driving or doing something that requires all your physical and mental faculties. Or continued drinking during ongoing legal issues. Or continued drinking in the presence of relational problems in which the drinking worsens the issue. If you have had one or more of these things present in your life within a 12-month period, it is likely you have an addiction to alcohol.

I would explain this to Tony and determine with him the level of his alcohol addiction. Tony used alcohol to cope with his life-threatening injuries from the shrapnel, to deal with the stress of his competitors and the constant demands from S.H.I.E.L.D. He drank to cope with his broken engagement, and his drinking worsened relational issues with his ex-fiancée and ex-girlfriend. It is safe to say Tony had a problem with alcohol. This brings up a secondary issue. Was Tony dependent on alcohol or did he abuse alcohol?

You may not know, but there is a difference between abuse and dependence upon a substance like alcohol. Here are the characteristics of dependence:

- **Craving**- An overwhelming desire to drink.
- **Loss of Control**- Drinking to excess without the ability to limit or stop.
- **Tissue Dependence**- A physiological need for the substance.
- **Tolerance**- Previous levels of consumption no longer achieve the same ends; therefore, more drinking is required to reach the same level of intoxication.
- **Withdrawal Symptoms**- Severe physical symptoms caused by the lack of drinking. These symptoms include: nausea, throwing up, excessive sweating, anxiety, shakiness, possibly seizures and even hallucinations (auditory and visual).

On the other hand, alcohol abuse does not have the same characteristics. Alcohol abuse is:

- **Moderate Cravings**- A desire to drink that can be controlled.
- **Moderate Loss of Control**- Limiting or stopping one's drinking is hard, but not impossible. One's level of drinking has a

negative impact on relationships, work and other responsibilities.

As you can see when looking at the two categories, there are some differences. Alcohol dependence is considered a *disease* by the medical field. That means, there is less choice and control regarding one's drinking. In the case of abuse, there is more choice and control. One abuses alcohol by choice, not due to a biological compulsion.

So, where does Tony land? Well, you have to think of issues with alcohol on a spectrum, alcohol dependence being one extreme, to total abstinence on the other end. Tony would probably fall somewhere between dependence and abuse. And if you pressed me, I'd say he abused alcohol, but wasn't dependent.

Therapy for Tony

What makes me say Tony abused alcohol, but wasn't dependent? Look at the evidence. Tony chose to drink to escape negative emotion. He didn't drink out of a physiological compulsion which would imply disease. Yet, it is the extreme level to which he drank that pushes him further down the spectrum. He drank to the point of losing two significant relationships. Also, he lost his business and his money; essentially, he lost everything. Here's the caveat, though: he was able to seek help, join a recovery group (AA), and successfully live the recovery lifestyle without seeking medical attention. Someone with alcohol dependence simply would not be able to do this even if they wanted to. They would need medical assistance.

The typical steps involved in the treatment of alcoholism are as follows: intervention, detoxification, and treatment.

- **Intervention** is the stage in which the alcoholic's denial no longer avoids the problem. A spouse leaves them or they lose their job, or family members get together to confront them. This is otherwise known as "hitting rock bottom": when things get their absolute worst and the alcoholic starts to reconsider their life and drinking.
- **Detoxification** is the second step, in which the alcoholic detoxifies under the monitoring and care of medical professions. In some cases, "detoxing" can be fatal if they try to do it on their own.

Therefore, it is necessary to have doctors and nurses to help during this stage.

- **Treatment** is the third step. This is when the alcoholic engages in the hard work of understanding their addiction, why they drink, what triggers their drinking, how their drinking has damaged them and the people around them: from here they can develop better strategies for dealing with the factors that lead them to drink. Most see addiction and alcoholism as a lifelong journey, so this step also involves joining a support group for the benefit of oneself and others.

Knowing what I know of Stark's history, I would point out that Tony used alcohol to escape from unpleasant emotions. At that time, he didn't know how to deal with things that didn't go his way. He was flooded with feelings that he didn't know how to cope with. As a result, he turned to alcohol to shut off his feelings. This is an effective short-term fix, but in the long run, it destroys lives. Tony had to address and handle his feelings. He couldn't afford to avoid them any longer.

Sometimes it takes hitting your "rock bottom." But that doesn't have to be you. If you struggle with addressing and handling your feelings, consider Tony an object lesson. The avoidance of emotions can lead to catastrophic effects. Don't let this be you. The following are 4 suggestions on how to handle emotions.

- **Seeking Understanding**: Instead of avoiding, try to understand why you are feeling what you are feeling. Look for a *trigger*—this is a term counselors use for the thing that initiated the feeling. For example, I had a client who would burst into tears every time he watched *Field of Dreams*. He didn't know why the movie affected him that way. I asked him to tell me about his dad. His father died before they could resolve some deep issues between them. He never told this to anyone because he was afraid to face the feelings of loss and regret. This realization was a turning point for him. He could never have made this progress without noticing the trigger.

- **Perspective**: Understand that emotions are your brain's way of alerting you to something that needs attention. Where there's smoke, there's fire. You wouldn't ignore blood streaming down your arm, would you? No, you'd immediately start looking for a wound so you could treat it. Healthy people treat emotions in the same way. Therefore, value your feelings.

- **Emotional Regulation Skills**: Refer back to the Silver Surfer chapter. Use skills to manage uncomfortable feelings like self-soothing, so that your feelings aren't in control, you are in control.

- **Don't Do It Alone**: Dealing with overwhelming, intense, painful emotions can be hard. Reach out to a trusted friend and share what you are going through. It's okay to be vulnerable and honest. In fact, it's really healthy and it feels good.

Tony hit his rock bottom. It was a wake-up call. He realized the way he was doing life wasn't working. This realization is half the battle. The next step is putting in the effort of working on yourself. No one wakes up an alcoholic. Alcoholics are made (some with a little help from nature). Tony abused alcohol for a reason. I would walk Tony through his major life events, helping him process each one, discuss triggers and teach emotional regulation skills. I'd recommend Tony continue attending groups to get support from others.

If you have a problem with alcohol, trying to fix the problem on your own is just about the worst thing you could do. You need other people. Those who live successful lives of recovery do it in community. Don't lone-wolf it. Tony thought he could handle the loss of his parents, the end of two significant relationships and stress at work by himself, but he couldn't. No one can. You are only as strong as your community. Surround yourself with supportive people who can hold you up when you can't stand on your own.

Adam Warlock

A scientifically created perfect human being, master of the Soul Gem, savior of Counter-Earth, one-time god, Adam Warlock wears many hats, making him one of the most complex characters in the Marvel Universe. Adam Warlock was created by a group of scientists called the Enclave. They hoped to create the perfect human in the hopes of exploiting him for their own purposes. While forming in a cocoon, Warlock became aware of their nefarious plot, broke free, and destroyed his creators. Although Warlock was an advanced being, he was not very mature. He was killed and revived after an altercation with Thor over a conflict regarding the Lady Sif (Thor's lover). This taught Warlock some needed maturity, but he still had far to go.

Fortunately, Warlock encountered the being the High Evolutionary.

The High Evolutionary was a human scientist who developed the ability to evolve or devolve himself or others. He tried to create perfect humanity out of animals to lead the way for utopia on Earth. Yet, the plan failed. He created Counter-Earth (a smaller recreated Earth on the opposite side of the Sun) as a second attempt at utopia. The plan was only to put highly evolved created human beings on Counter-Earth, thus eliminating evil. Again, the plan went awry.

A being called Man-Beast, another creation of the High Evolutionary, took over and corrupted Counter-Earth with his own special brand of evil. Warlock pleaded with the High Evolutionary to spare Counter-Earth and allow him to live on it. He agreed and gave him the Soul Gem. The Soul Gem is one of six Gems that when collected, form the Infinity Gauntlet. An item that grants godhood to its possessor. Reminiscent of the biblical account of the Passion, Warlock was crucified and resurrected, and defeated Man-Beast. A religion was established to worship Warlock. Adam didn't stay to enjoy the adulation of Counter-Earth. He certainly could have taken advantage of the situation, yet he refused the god status available for the taking.

This is where the story gets a bit complicated. In an alternate future,[18]Adam goes insane and become the Magus. Magus is an ego-maniacal self-defined god who wants nothing more than the total domination of the universe. In a twist of fate, this future Magus is thrust back in time. He begins his following, the Universal Church of Truth. A "Church" that forcibly indoctrinates people. The Church grows in its power and domination over planets and people. However, the Church is cruel and uses its power for evil purposes, which gets the attention of Warlock and Thanos. However, they are attentive to the Church for different reasons. Warlock wants to help and protect people by defending them from the Church. Thanos sees the Church as a legitimate threat to his own power and dominion.

Thanos and Warlock find themselves to be odd bedfellows and team up to fight the Magus, though in defeating him, Thanos had ulterior motives for helping Warlock. He used the

---

[18] In Marvel, there are numerous alternate realities and time streams.

opportunity to wrest Soul Gem from Warlock while obtaining the other five Gems, thus wielding the Infinity Gauntlet. The wearer is granted omnipotence: in other words, whoever wears the Infinity Gauntlet becomes God. But godhood isn't cracked up to what seems to be. Thanos struggled to master his new-found powers. Warlock and a team of superheroes manage to get the Gauntlet from Thanos, effectively saving the universe.

Adam, now in possession of the gauntlet, makes his best effort at being God, but quickly realizes that his good and dark sides are at war with each other. In order to remove the impediment of good and evil, he splits himself into three beings: his good side, the Goddess; his dark side, the Magus; and Warlock, the logical, impartial, dispassionate side keeps control of the gauntlet. Warlock's extreme measures did little to win the confidence of the other cosmic beings. The Living Tribunal[19] orders him to separate the

---

[19] The Living Tribunal is a cosmic being who makes judgments on the One-Above-All's behalf. He is the decider and enforcer of the One-Above-All's will. The One-Above-All is the creator of the multiverse. The One-Above-All is Marvel's version of God whereas DC's version of God is The Presence. A personal side note, if Warlock were truly God, how can he be divested

Gems, never to be used in conjunction again. Warlock distributes the five Gems (keeping his original Gem, the Soul Gem) to Gamora, Drax the Destroyer, Pip the Troll, Moondragon, and Thanos. It is, however, Warlock's choice to split himself into three entities that opens the universe to danger for a second and third time. The Magus makes a second attempt at taking over the universe and nearly succeeds. He is defeated and sent to Soulworld. Then the Goddess attempts to cleanse all corruption from the universe, meaning the annihilation of all living beings. She nearly succeeds, but is defeated by Warlock and a team of superheroes. Warlock accepts his mistake of cleaving his good and bad side and reintegrates them into his being.

Wellbeing for Warlock

Where would I start if Warlock walked into my office looking for counseling? One could make the case that Adam, by choice, suffered from DID, *Dissociative Identity Disorder*. This is the updated

---

of his power by the Living Tribunal? Wouldn't the Living Tribunal be working for Warlock at that point?

clinical term for MPD, *Multiple Personality Disorder.*

DID is a psychological condition in which a person has two or more identities or personality states. There is much debate regarding the cause and nature of the disorder. For some time, the public and mental health professionals believed clients suffering from DID were faking it. They thought clients manufactured their symptoms in an elaborate ruse to get attention. However, the more DID has been researched, the more this assertion has been proven false. There is simply too much evidence against the "faking it" hypothesis. For example, when another identity takes over—let's refer to it as a "secondary identity"—the secondary identity possesses characteristics that are unlike the primary identity. And the differences are not minor. The differences include facial appearance and expression, right- or left-handedness, memory, language, and dialect. Furthermore, the primary identity has a memory gap when the secondary identity is in control. This data really has clinicians and diagnosticians scratching their heads. So, what are some explanations for this data?

Some firmly believe that there are multiple identities or personalities residing in one person. How this happens, they don't know. Why it happens, they don't know. The human mind is complex and mysterious. Possibly, the mind records more information than we are aware of, on a subconscious level. If true, theoretically the mind could assemble a second personality out of information passively gathered. The strength of this view is its acknowledgment of mystery. And there is indeed a great deal of mystery when it comes to the human mind. The weakness of this view: our subconscious minds aren't like a running tape recorder. People don't unknowingly record information and then for some unknown reason, collate that information into a separate identity. At least, there is no empirical evidence for this.

In the second view, multiple independent identities are evidence for the *Collective Unconscious*. If you are open to unexplained spiritual realities in the universe, this view may appeal to you. Carl Jung, the famous Swiss psychiatrist, and founder of analytical psychology, was a student of Sigmund Freud. In many ways Jung followed in his teacher's intellectual footsteps, yet he diverged from Freud regarding the unconscious. Jung believed that human behavior, thoughts, and feelings are driven by *archetypes*. These archetypes are stored in the *collective unconscious*. In order to understand these concepts, think of a web-based cloud service that everyone is linked to. This cloud is a repository of templates for human behavior collected over the span of human history. Unconsciously, these stored templates (my paraphrase for archetypes) inform and shape human behavior. But Jung's "cloud" is mystical instead of digital. And you thought that Jung was just the guy who came up with *introversion* and *extroversion*! Jung was a mystic, occultist, spiritualist—in addition to being a brilliant psychiatrist.

The third view is the fragmentation explanation. That is to say, as a result of trauma, an organic brain issue, Schizophrenia or an unidentified factor, a client's personality will fragment into many different pieces. There is a lot of clinical support for this idea. In some cases, particular identities will predictably emerge under certain circumstances. For example, if a client with DID is put in a threatening situation, their "protector identity" will take over. Or, when they are hurting emotionally, their "victim identity" will take over and express all the wounds and hurts the primary identity has suffered. There are recorded cases where the fragmented identities have an awareness of each other. At times, the secondary and tertiary identities could be critical, protective and/or at conflict with each other. For empirical support, researchers have done brain imaging when a client has transitioned from identity to identity. An entirely different brain profile of activity emerges after the transition. This lends a great deal of verifiable, observable data for this view. Taking all of this data and evidence into account, it is easy to see why this is the most popular view. If this view is true, the clinical goal for clients suffering from DID is reintegration of the fragmented identities (more on this later). This is compelling evidence in support of the fragmentation view, yet this view has no explanation for secondary and tertiary identities that are completely separate from the primary identity. That is to say, they aren't fragments, but independent identities.

So how does DID come into this discussion about the collective unconscious? If you agree with Jung, it's not a far leap to think whole identities exist in the collective unconscious—

identities that could possibly channel through a living person. Interesting as this view may be, there are little to none who hold it, for its simple lack of empirical evidence.

Treatment for DID

The commonly accepted view in the field of psychology is that DID is caused by a fragmentation of someone's identity due to: traumatic experience, or a genetic disorder that runs in families, or schizophrenia, or, an organic brain disorder. The goal of treatment is to make the client aware of their various identities in the hopes of reintegrating the fragments. Clients who suffer from DID, typically, also struggle with depression, anxiety, and PTSD. Therefore, treatment of Adam Warlock would focus on reintegration of the fragmented identities.

As we know from Warlock's story, *Infinity Crusade*[20] ends with Warlock reintegrating the Goddess and Magus into himself. He reconciles the fact that there is an internal struggle between our good and bad, dark and light sides. This is not

---

[20] The final part in the three-part saga where the Goddess is the primary enemy that Warlock must face.

far off from what we would do in counseling. By treating Warlock, I would hope to create awareness of his other identities. Through understanding them, he can then accept them as sometimes conflicting parts of himself. We all struggle with some internal conflicts. For example, someone wants to lose weight, but they love Twinkies. Those two parts of the self that are at war: one side, the responsible health-conscious side, wants to be healthier and lose weight; the other side, the indulgent, gluttonous side, loves Twinkies and wants to keep eating Twinkies. This is true of decisions in life. Do I drop out of school to travel? Do I marry this person or someone else? Do I rip this person off to make money?

Internal conflicts are normal. They are an inescapable reality of being human. Internal conflicts do create a lot of problems, but on the upside, they also provide confirmation of human freedom. You are able to make choices—for or against—despite having strong desires for a particular option. This can be troubling for some, but if you think about it, it's actually quite empowering. You have the ability to make choices. You aren't destined to live a life of depression or anxiety. You can choose to live the life you want. For some, all they need to make is the choice; for others, they need to make the choice and get extra help. But the need for help doesn't nullify the power of one's choice. If there wasn't an internal conflict, that would mean you could only make one choice, or there was only one voice directing your choices. Is that free will, or the life of an automaton? Well, I'll leave those questions for the theologians and philosophers.

Warlock couldn't accept the internal battle, so he chose to split his being. But once he was able to accept the conflicting sides of himself, he was then able to reintegrate. This is the beauty and compelling nature of Warlock's story. He raises fascinating philosophical questions while giving key insights into human nature. He shows us that internal conflicts are normal. Yet, we can still choose to do the right thing, the healthy thing. We have the power to influence the course of our lives through choices.

Magneto

Auschwitz survivor, mutant, leader, friend of Charles Xavier: that's right, it's Magneto – one of the most feared and powerful of all mutants. Magneto is charming, intelligent, ruggedly handsome, philosophically inclined, but a man of action. All these things make Magneto an interesting character, but what makes his story compelling is a fantasy grounded in reality. Born Max Eisenhardt, Magneto watched his family murdered at the hands of Nazis, then was sent to Auschwitz prison camp. There, he joined the *Sonderkommando*, a squad of Jewish men who were forced to operate the gas chambers, ovens and fire pits. After Magneto survived the prison camp with a woman named Magda, whom he married and had three children with, he made his way to Israel. Along the way,

Max's first daughter died in a tragic fire. Max, grief-stricken, abandons his wife and continues his travels to Israel. This was a tragic decision since, unbeknownst to him, his wife was pregnant with twins. She died while giving birth to the twins coincidentally when Max fatefully meets Charles Xavier in Israel.

After getting to know each other, the two quickly realized each other were mutants. They became friends and debated the finer points of mutant-human relations. Max considered mutants to be a superior race; he called his race *homo sapiens superior*. He believed that humanity was morally corrupt, based on his experiences in the Nazi prison camp, and felt that mutants were the next step in the evolutionary chain. He admitted the next step in the progress of evolution would likely be a violent one. Xavier, on the other hand, had a different perspective. He believed mutants and humans could live in peace with each other. Mutant powers were a gift that should be used for good purposes.

The fundamental and irreconcilable differences between the two were apparent to Max, prompting him to take his leave of Xavier. He left to create a mutant force in the hopes of preventing another holocaust, and to establish a mutant homeland. He formed the Brotherhood of Mutants and took on the persona of Magneto. Xavier went on to create the X-Men. The two would square off on the battlefield. What once was a friendly disagreement would become the fodder of a bitter rivalry.

Magneto's plan was to eradicate Earth of humanity. Xavier and the X-Men defended humanity in a series of battles between the two groups. Each conflict would end in Magneto's apparent death. However, each time Magneto managed to avoid death. Again and again, he would muster his forces to attack humanity. Dastardly though he may be, Magneto is a survivor. But even the best of us have bad days. Even the best of us lose heart and succumb to discouragement. This begs the question, how does one be *resilient* in the face of loss, defeat and disappointment?

Meaning for Magneto

Let's suppose Magneto has one of those "off-days." He's defeated once more by the X-Men and instead of bouncing back like he always does, something holds him back. He's tired of spinning his wheels on a fruitless effort. He calls me on the phone and wants a session. What would I do to help Magneto?

I would first explain to Magneto what resilience is and then go from there. In the immortal words of Vince Lombardi, "It's not whether you get knocked down, it's whether you get back up." Sure, we all like the idea of getting back up, but how many of us really do it? Trust me, when life pushes you down, it's really hard to keep fighting. Life can certainly feel like a dream-crushing machine sometimes. So, what's the secret of resilience? What is it that makes a person bounce back from defeat?

Resilience defined is the ability to overcome obstacles, personal tragedy, and trauma by adapting. It's not a superpower that only the extraordinary have. Ordinary people live lives of resilience. Jobs are lost, family members die, investments don't turn out: this kind of thing happens every day. And every day, ordinary people adapt, change and keep going. To not adapt, change and go on leaves you stuck. Now, I'm not saying just because its ordinary, it's easy. It's really hard to adapt to change. But it's entirely within your power to do so. It just takes some work. Here are 10 ways you can build resilience in your life:[21]

- **Make connections.** Good relationships with close family members, friends or others are important. Accepting help and support from those who care about you and will listen to you strengthens resilience. Some people find that being active in civic groups, faith-based organizations, or other local groups provide social support and can help with reclaiming hope. Assisting others in their time of need, also, can benefit the helper.

- **Avoid seeing crises as insurmountable problems.** You can't change the fact that highly stressful events happen, but you can change how you interpret and respond to these events. Try looking beyond the present to how future circumstances may be a little better. Note any subtle ways in which you might already feel somewhat better as you deal with difficult situations.

- **Accept that change is a part of living.** Certain goals may no longer be

[21] American Psychological Association: http://www.apa.org/helpcenter/road-resilience.aspx. Retrieval date: January, 18th, 2016.

attainable as a result of adverse situations. Accepting circumstances that cannot be changed can help you focus on circumstances that you can alter.

- **Move toward your goals.** Develop some realistic goals. Do something regularly – even if it seems like a small accomplishment – that enables you to move toward your goals. Instead of focusing on tasks that seem unachievable, ask yourself, "What's one thing I know I can accomplish today that helps me move in the direction I want to go?"

- **Take decisive actions.** Act on adverse situations as much as you can. Take decisive actions, rather than detaching completely from problems and stresses and wishing they would just go away.

- **Look for opportunities for self-discovery.** People often learn something about themselves and may find that they have grown in some respect as a result of their struggle with loss. Many people who have experienced tragedy and hardship have reported better relationships, a greater sense of strength even while feeling vulnerable, increased sense of self-worth, a more developed spirituality, and heightened appreciation for life.

- **Nurture a positive view of yourself.** Developing confidence in your ability to solve problems and trusting your instincts will help in building resilience.
- **Keep things in perspective.** Even when facing very painful events, try to consider the stressful situation in a broader context and keep a long-term perspective. Avoid blowing the event out of proportion.
- **Maintain a hopeful outlook.** An optimistic outlook enables you to expect that good things will happen in your life. Try visualizing what you want, rather than worrying about what you fear.
- **Take care of yourself.** Pay attention to your own needs and feelings. Engage in activities that you enjoy and find relaxing. Exercise regularly. Taking care of yourself helps to keep your mind and body primed to deal with situations that require resilience.
- **Additional ways of strengthening resilience may be helpful.** For example, some people write about their deepest thoughts and feelings related to trauma or

other stressful events in their life. Meditation and spiritual practices help some people build connections and restore hope.

Reviewing these ten steps may boost Magneto's resilience. I would remind him of all the things he's overcome. He survived Auschwitz, he became a father and has two amazing kids (Quicksilver and Scarlet Witch), he's reconnected with his old friend Xavier, he's become one of the most powerful mutants, and he's looked upon by many as a leader. Not to mention, he's returned from apparently dying more times than I can count. He is truly a survivor, but is surviving enough? Resilience is the ability to move from surviving to thriving. In order to do this, Magneto needs to keep in mind that he's overcome so much *in the past* and he can continue to overcome obstacles *in the future*.

But what if Magneto takes my advice, doesn't that create a dilemma? What if Magneto's resilience is boosted and he returns to his master plan to vanquish humanity? By helping him I've put humanity at risk. Resilience is a powerful personal quality to possess, and anyone can have it. Jesus said in the New Testament "He causes his sun to rise on the evil and the good, and sends rain on the righteous and the unrighteous."[22] In other words, there's equal opportunity for good or evil men to have resilience.

The Dark and Light Side of Resilience

Resilience is an incredible personal quality to have. Most of our culture's real-life heroes are recognized as being resilient. One such hero, Martin Luther King Jr., lead three walks from Selma to Montgomery during the Civil Rights Movement. This was a protest march organized to highlight racial inequality in the United States during the 1950's and 60's. The first of the three marches was considered an abysmal failure. It was called *Bloody Sunday* because protesters were brutally beaten by the police. This greatly discouraged others to protest and was a setback for the movement. However, Martin Luther King Jr. was the definition of resilient. He attempted the march a second and third time. On the third march, President Lyndon B. Johnson protected the protesters when Governor George Wallace refused. This gave national recognition and presidential support, which was a much needed

---

[22] Matthew 5:45, NIV.

boost for a struggling cause. Martin Luther King Jr. shows us the positive side of resilience. He had a vision for what the world could be. And when he encountered setbacks, failures and disappointments, they hurt, but they did not stop him. Resilience can be an unstoppable force, but what if an evil person had the same kind of resilience King had? Is there a dark side to resilience?

One could argue that Joseph Stalin was a resilient individual. He had a vision for a utopian society. However, in order to craft his utopia out of the then Soviet Union, he had to crave away sections of his own population. This "craving" was atrocious, brutal and vicious. Stalin killed, imprisoned, and deported millions of people. Deaths that can be directly attributed to his regime range from 4 million to 60 million. However, most historians agree on 20 million deaths. [23] Stalin makes Hitler's atrocities look meager in comparison.

Stalin grew up in a poor family. As a young man he entered seminary and was kicked out for

---

[23] http://historyofrussia.org/stalin-killed-how-many-people/.
Retrieval Date: Sept. 6th, 2016.

missing exams. As an adult Stalin was arrested several times for political and criminal activities. When he married, first wife died from Typhus and his second wife committed suicide.[24] Despite all these setbacks, Stalin resiliently pursued his vision, which ensured the death of millions upon millions of people. To put it another way, his tenacity, his resolve, and resilience in the face of failure guaranteed the death of 20 million people. Thanks a lot resilience. Therefore, the moral of the story is that resilience can be used for good *or* evil. Resilience is a quality that can absolutely make your life better, but does it also come with a moral responsibility?

Resilience Boost

If you are also having an off-day and feeling like you could use a resilience boost, do the same thing I just did with Magneto. Look back over your life and review the obstacles you've overcome. I bet there are more victories than you give yourself credit for. Keep those victories in mind: think about the skills, strengths, talents, and resources you used. Write them down on a

---

[24] http://www.history.com/topics/joseph-stalin. Retrieval Date: Sept. 7th, 2016.

piece of paper. Now, think about how you can use those same assets, but with the new obstacle. That doesn't mean you have to use them in the same way though—same tool, different context, different application. How you use a tool differs from problem to problem. This is where you have to be flexible.

Let me give you an example. I once worked with a man who recently had a stroke. The motor skills of one side of his body were impaired. And he was feeling depressed about the loss. Through getting to know him better, I learned he was a master gardener. Out of curiosity, I asked him how he got into gardening. Several years prior, the client and his wife had moved into a new area. They loved the house, but the backyard was a total mess. My client knew next to nothing about gardening or landscaping. He took it upon himself to learn everything there was to know about horticulture, lawn care, and gardening. Ten years later, he was a master gardener and his backyard was in better shape. But more importantly, gardening gave my client purpose.

I wondered what was it that transformed him from knowing nothing about lawn care and gardening to having a whole new life purpose. He paused for a moment, looked back at me and said, "Curiosity." It was his curiosity that motivated him to learn, struggle and ultimately master his lawn and garden. It was his curiosity that gave him pleasure, passion and purpose. I asked him if his curiosity could be of help to him with this new obstacle. He chuckled to himself and said, "Yes, it absolutely can."

For my client, there was a lot of work ahead. Recovery meant a long period of physical therapy, and even then, he might not fully recover. He was also going to have to make some serious lifestyle changes. He was going to need other people more. This was humbling, scary and hard, but not impossible. Yet, what gave my client the motivation, courage and strength to do what he needed to do was his curiosity. In the following months, my client learned everything there was to know about strokes. He read, studied and he worked his butt off. Recovering from a stroke was like taming his overgrown, messy yard. Yes, there were some dark days and setbacks, but he persevered.

Resiliency is a lifestyle that you can learn. At whatever stage of life you are in, you will be faced with loss, challenge and difficulty.

Challenges have a way of fooling people into thinking things are hopeless. That simply is a lie. You've overcome challenges before and you can overcome challenges now. Follow the ten steps to build resilience in your life. Take a page out of my client's playbook and use the skills you've learned past experiences in new contexts. And hopefully, you won't follow in the footsteps of Stalin or Magneto. But, there is hope for Magneto yet. His counterpart Professor Xavier is also an example of resilience. With my counseling and Xavier's friendship, we may yet redirect his resilience along a path that benefits both humans and mutants. I just won't wear anything metallic to our sessions.

Gamora

Abandoned baby, adopted daughter of Thanos, assassin, Time Gem keeper, and member of the Infinity Watch—that's right, we're talking about the green-skinned seductress, Gamora. Bad girl turned good. She is as lethal as she is beautiful. But her beginning isn't as sexy as you would think. The Universal Church of Truth slaughtered an innocent race, the Zen-Whoberi, leaving an abandoned baby in their wake. Thanos took the baby in as his own. He named her Gamora.

Thanos wasn't your typical parent. That is to say, most parents don't treat their kids like science experiments, but that's exactly what Thanos did to Gamora. He used a machine to alter her body so that she would be an adult in peak physical condition. He also used the machine to create a "mental block" in her mind so that she could not see his evil. In this state, she was compliant to his commands. Her first mission: infiltrate the Universal Church of Truth for the purposes of creating chaos and assassinating the Magus (Adam Warlock's evil, future self). She teamed up with Warlock to defeat the Magus, however, when she returned home to Thanos, the mental veil had been lifted and she saw Thanos for who he really was, evil. She rebelled against him, which would turn out to be a life-threatening decision. Thanos attacks and mortally wounds his adopted daughter. Fortunately, Warlock finds her on the brink of death and preserves her soul in his Soul Gem. She returns to her body later on when Thanos acquires the Infinity Gauntlet. After that, she teamed up with Warlock, takes possession of the Time Gem, and served as an Infinity Watch member, defending the universe against Warlock's alter-egos.

After many battles, the Infinity Watch disbands, and then Gamora does something very surprising: she returns to Thanos. She not only returns to him, she aids him in his plotting, scheming, and missions. Gamora eventually goes on to do other things like leading a group of female cosmic warriors and joining the Guardians of the Galaxy. But the question still nags: why did Gamora return and help Thanos?

Gamora has every reason to hate Thanos. Yes, he did rescue her after the Universal Church of Truth wiped out the Zen-Whoberi, but he did so with ulterior motives. Thanos rescued Gamora with the intention of experimenting on and using her for his own selfish purposes. Additionally, he brainwashed her so that she couldn't see his evil. Not to mention, he mortally wounded her, forcing Warlock to save her life with the use of the Soul Gem. Why in the world would she go back to him?! Let's suppose Gamora walks into my office wondering the same thing. She's as baffled as I am about why she went back.

Getting Help for Gamora

Although Gamora's behavior may not be rational, that doesn't mean it isn't normal. Human beings do irrational things all the time. Alternatively, there may indeed be an explanation for Gamora's return to Thanos. Let's consider a few options and then decide which one is most likely.

Theory #1: Gamora was Brainwashed!

In the 1950's, after the Korean War, the US military invested a great deal of focus into the science of mind control. Why? After the war finished, 21 US soldiers who were held captive refused to return home. They decided to defect and join the communist cause. This made the military suspect they were under the influence of mind control.

The field of psychology doesn't use the term mind control or brainwashing. The term that is used is *thought reform*. Thought reform is broken down into three subcategories: compliance, persuasion, and education. Compliance focuses on influencing and changing another's behavior. Persuasion focuses on influencing or changing another's attitude and/or mindset. Education (or propaganda) aims at influencing, shaping and/or changing one's beliefs or belief system. As you can see, when broken down into these three categories, brainwashing isn't as effective as it's made out to be. What is *really* meant discussing brainwashing is *social influence*. And social influence happens every day in all sorts of ways.

Let's look at what happened to Gamora through the lens of the three subcategories of thought reform. At first, Gamora was controlled through persuasion. Then, like I said before, Thanos used a machine to alter her perceptions so that she couldn't see his evil. This enabled Thanos to give Gamora commands, which she followed (she infiltrated the Universal Church of Truth on a mission to assassinate the Magus). However, Warlock helped Gamora counteract the mental block, thus freeing her from Thanos' control. She rebelled against Thanos and joined his enemies. So now, you'd think she'd want nothing to do with her adopted father? This makes the second return to Thanos all the more mysterious. Thanos no longer had the machine implant to control her. So, how did he get her to come back?

Theory #2: Gamora Suffered from Stockholm Syndrome.

Jump two decades ahead from the Korean War to the 1970's. In 1973, there was a six-day bank robbery / hostage negotiation / police standoff in Stockholm, Sweden. But this bank robbery was like no other. Over the course of the six days, the bank employees—held as captives—formed an attachment to their captors as evidenced by declining help from the police and even defending their captors after being freed. This bizarre behavior manifested was later coined *Stockholm Syndrome*.

The way psychologists make sense of this strange reaction of a captive to their captor has to do with trauma. Traumatic experiences have a way of bonding people together, even captive to captor, which of course is odd because the captive is bonding with the person creating their trauma. But this nonetheless happens. The bonding that occurs between people during or after a trauma has been observed in soldiers, natural disaster victims, family members after the death of a loved one, abused women bound to their abusive partners, abused children to their abusive parents, rape victims to their rapists, and finally, people who have been kidnapped to their kidnappers. Needless to say, trauma bonds people together like glue and you don't get to choose who the glue sticks you with.

So, could Gamora have trauma-bonded with Thanos? He did, after all, inflict quite a bit of trauma on her. He altered her body and mind, used her as an assassin and mortally wounded her. Not the most loving father figure, is he? This option is entirely likely.

Theory #3: Thanos was Abusive and Controlling; Gamora was Psychologically Controlled by Thanos.

You may be wondering, what's the difference between Theory 1 and Theory 3? There is in fact a difference between thought reform and psychological control. Psychological control is multifaceted and it's usually seen in abusive, intimate relationships. It begins with the abuser persuading the victim to the think they are utterly helpless without their abuser—that they are defenseless and wouldn't survive without him.[25] The abuser then systematically cuts their victim off from resources like friends, family members, money, transportation, and job. If the victim has no contact with anyone other than their abuser, no one can advocate for her, help her or provide outside influence. The abuser wants only their

---

[25] In this section I use the male pronoun for the abuser and the female pronoun for the victim. Statistically speaking, men represent the majority of abusers in intimate relationships and women represent the majority of victims.

voice, their influence and their will to dominate the victim. Things will eventually get so bad that the victim wants to leave, but they can't, since they've come to believe they are utterly helpless without their abuser. They believe the lie that they aren't capable of leaving or standing up for themselves. Psychological control is about suppressing someone's will so that the abuser can have control.

There is some overlap between psychological control and Stockholm Syndrome in that the victim feels an emotional bond and allegiance to the abuser/captor. So what differentiates the two from each other? Psychological control is usually systematic, long-term, intended to control an intimate partner, and is done to fulfill a need of the abuser. Let me repeat since it bears some importance, the abuser is fulfilling a psychological need through the abuse. With Stockholm Syndrome, control may happen incidentally. The captor may not intend for the psychological control and subsequent bonding to occur, but, due to the traumatic and intimacy inducing nature of the crime, it happens. If the captor does intend to create psychological control in their captive, it would likely be done to fulfill an objective of his or her mission and not to fulfill a need.

Regarding Gamora, theory #3 is entirely possible. Thanos is abusive, manipulative, evil and very powerful. He almost killed her, but he didn't. He simply wanted her to know that he could. He wanted her to think she will always be in danger from him. This is another tactic of abusers I didn't mention above. Abusers will threaten their victims if they ever try to get away. They give their victims one of two options: stay and be "safe" (not really safe, more like controlled) or, flee and be harmed by the abuser himself. This is not an empty threat. Abused women are more likely to be killed by their male partner relative to a person killed by other means. Abused women makes on average 7 attempts to leave before they are able to leave permanently. However, attempting to leave can be dangerous. 75% of abused women are murdered at the hands of their partner when they attempt to leave. Roughly 4000 women die every year at the hands of their abusive partners![26] After Gamora rebelled

---

26

http://www.domesticabuseshelter.org/infodomesticviolence. htm. Retrieval January, 21st, 2016. These statistics are a bit and joined Warlock, the fear could have been growing in the back of her mind: "Thanos could take revenge for my betrayal at any moment." So, she runs back to him where she knows she's safe from his retribution.

Theories and Therapy

Okay, we've discussed the three theories that possibly explain Gamora's return to Thanos. Now, which one is it? One could argue that all three theories are at play. Maybe Gamora was subjected to thought reform. Maybe she was suffering from Stockholm Syndrome, and maybe she was psychologically controlled. All three could be operating in her psyche at the same time. A mix of all three is most likely the case. Thanos "brainwashed" Gamora through the use of his machine. He also traumatized and thus bonded with her by killing Gamora's parents and people group, and kidnapping her. And, one could argue, by mortally wounding Gamora, she was the victim of Domestic Violence and Abuse. He was, after all, a father figure to her. What kind of father

---

dated, therefore, there may be more accurate numbers available.

beats his child? Thanos was not a good father by any stretch of the imagination and all his actions were done for the purpose of using and controlling Gamora. Gamora's story, although a fictional story, isn't far off from what happens in real life. She can serve as an example to us.

If you are in an abusive relationship and you want things to stop, you must first confront your own psychological control. You will never be physically free unless you are psychologically free. I would recommend seeing a counselor, reconnecting with friends, family and co-workers who can listen, support and advocate for you. Read books, watch YouTube videos, TV specials, and listen to podcasts on domestic violence and abuse. Look into local shelters and advocacy groups in your area. You can set yourself free from abuse, but you will need the help of others. Don't live your life in fear. Surround yourself with a community that can help.

If you know someone who is in an abusive relationship and you're frustrated as to why they won't leave, take the time to try and understand. Even though you can't see psychological control, believe me, it's there and it's powerful. It's strong enough to keep an abused person in the environment of abuse. Be a friend and a listener. You could even share the story of Gamora with them. She did, after all, leave Thanos. For many women, it may take up to seven attempts before they successfully leave the abusive relationship.[27] Remember, abused women are more likely to be killed by their abusive partner when attempting to leave. The fear abused women face is real. Fear is not an excuse to stay. You can be their advocate. You can be their lifeline.

---

[27] Ibid.

Black Adam

Teth-Adam, the counterpart to Captain Marvel, an ancient Egyptian prince, Black Adam is a super-villain and sometimes antihero who managed to survive several millennia. He is a human being with godlike powers, primarily concerned with his own supremacy. Black Adam is a force to be reckoned with.

Teth-Adam was an ancient Egyptian prince gifted with supernatural powers from the wizard Shazam. Teth-Adam merely has to say the magic word "Shazam" and a lightning bolt comes down from heaven, strikes Teth, and transforms him into Mighty Adam, a being of great power. Shazam chose Teth-Adam, after observing his moral purity, to become his predecessor. Yet,

Teth-Adam proved to be a regretful choice on Shazam's part. "Power corrupts, absolute power corrupts absolutely" holds true when it comes to Teth-Adam's case. The Egyptian prince's hunger for power extended over the entire world. He killed the Pharaoh and assumed the throne. Shazam seeing the evil of Teth-Adam renamed him "Black Adam" and was unable to take back the power given to him. He does, however, banish him to a planet in the farthest reach of the universe. Black Adam spends the next 5000 years flying back to Earth only to find he's been replaced by Shazam three times over. Shazam gifted three others the same power: Captain Marvel, Mary Marvel, and Captain Marvel Jr. Enraged by this turn of events, Black Adam tries to take over the world again. A battle ensues between Black Adam and the Marvel Family. Black Adam takes the upper hand, but is tricked by Uncle Marvel into reverting to his human form, thus allowing 5000 years of aging to hit him at once. He shrivels and dies on the spot, leaving a dusty skeleton.

30 years later Dr. Sivana, Captain Marvel's archenemy, resurrects Black Adam to continue their cause against the superhero family. In an

alternative origin story, Black Adam murders the family of Billy Batson, leaving him an orphan. Shazam sees Batson's plight and makes him his second champion, giving him the same Shazam powers as Black Adam. He takes the mantle of Captain Marvel and becomes a superhero. Black Adam eventually forms his own Black Marvel Family including his wife Isis and his brother Osiris, ruling and protecting their own kingdom, Kahndaq. Black Adam also joins various superhero and super-villain groups such as Justice Society of America (JSA), Injustice Society, Secret Society of Super-Villains, Suicide Squad, and the Monster Society of Evil.

To illustrate Adam's flip-flopping, at one point he teams up with Captain Marvel, including the Marvel Family and the JSA. At another time, Black Adam is a freedom fighter for his homeland, Kahndaq. He takes over with the help of a militia made of super-villains and JSA members. The coup works and Black Adam becomes the leader and protector of Kahndaq. Then, Kahndaq comes under attack and Black Adam blames the JSA. He then joins the Secret Society of Super-Villains in an effort to return fire.

Furthermore, his rule of Kahndaq isn't so nice. Adam considered himself ruler, guardian, and god of his original birth place. He established draconian laws. And televised executions of criminals every Wednesday which he carried out himself. His lethality caused a rift between him and the superhero community in the United States. Sensing the tension and fearing U.S. superheroes, Black Adam forms a coalition of powerful beings against the United States. Yet, the formation of this coalition would be his undoing. The coalition, called the Intergang, view Adam as a liability and create Sobek, the fourth of horsemen of Apokolips to kill the Black Marvels. Sobek manages to kill Osiris. The other three members of the horsemen kill Isis. Black Adam seeks revenge, yet his rage is blind. He kills indiscriminatingly anyone who obstructs his pursuit of Sobek, even going so far as to kill an entire population of 2 million. And did I mention, he goes on to start World War III?

The Blurred Lines of Black Adam

I mention all this like a lightning bolt (get the pun?) to demonstrate Black Adam's equivocation when it comes to siding with evil or good. In the beginning, he was quite virtuous. Shazam gave him powers because he saw purity of moral character. Yet, upon receiving power, Mighty Adam transformed into the corrupt and power-hungry, murderous Black Adam. After returning to Earth, he tried killing the Marvel family. Then had a change of heart and sided with the good guys. Then he swaps sides and teams up with super-criminals. Other times he doesn't even care whose side he's on, he just wants power. While in Kahndaq, he executes swift justice in his land, which is good, but there's no legal system, no due process, no presumption of innocence. And he's not meting out justice then throwing the criminals in jail. He personally kills those deemed criminal on public television. Then, to make matters worse, he launches World War III. His anger burns at everyone. He unleashes a wave of destruction upon the entire world. Hence, you may be wondering if Black Adam is a morally mixed up good guy, an opportunistic bad guy (siding with good when it aligns with his goals) or, a mix of good and bad, but one who really loves power?

Views of Morality

What do you think? Are people basically good or evil? Believe it or not, it is your assumption that informs how you perceive the facts. There are three positions to consider when it comes to the moral nature of mankind. They are:

- **People are Basically Good.** If you think people are basically good, then Teth-Adam was a good person corrupted by power. It wasn't him doing evil; it was the power influencing him. It was an outside force invading and changing an otherwise good person. Yet, this view raises some tricky questions. What is it about power that usually corrupts people? If people are good then why don't they use power for good?

- **People are Basically Evil.** If you think people are basically evil then Teth-Adam's actions after receiving power from Shazam make perfect sense. Adam was evil, therefore he used his power in an evil way. But what about his actions before receiving the power? The only reason Shazam gave him power in the first place was because he saw goodness in him. So much goodness that Shazam wanted him as a replacement. Furthermore, Black Adam did side with good after returning to Earth. He even teamed up with his enemy Captain Marvel. He's also very protective of his homeland Kahndaq. How do these good actions fit with someone who's basically evil?

- **People are a Mixture of Good and Bad and are Influenced by Good and Bad.** A wordy title, but you get the point. This view holds that people are a mix of good and bad. What influences our choices to do good or evil is background, community, world events, personal views, family views, religious views, books, the economy, biology, culture. These things pull in one direction or another, but they do not determine our choices. For Black Adam, he started out good, but power influenced him. He liked power and was willing to do anything to get more of it. As a result, he made evil choices. However, Black Adam reconsidered his evil choices and sided with good. But that didn't last for long. Power beckoned to him like a siren. He sided with whoever would aid him in his quest for power.

Who can say which view is right? Which view accurately describes the human condition? Are people basically good or evil, or somewhere in between? Let's see if social science can shed any light on the subject.

Stanley Milgram was a famous psychologist at Yale who conducted an experiment in the 1960's to test how obedience to authority influences the moral actions of people. The experiment was simple. The test subject would come into a room and ask a person in another room a series of "true or false" questions. Whenever the person got a question wrong, the subject had to administer an electric shock. The person receiving the shock (this was an actor who was not actually being shocked) would cry out in pain and plead the subject to stop. Often, after hearing the cries of pain coming from the other room, the subject would protest, question or refuse to go further with the study, but was urged on by the experimenter to continue. The debate would go on, but eventually, the subject would administer increasingly dangerous levels of shock to the other person. Milgram concluded in his study that people will obey morally atrocious orders when given by an authority figure.

Another researcher in the 1970's, psychologist Phillip Zimbardo, conducted the famous Stanford Prison studies in order to understand the moral nature of mankind. Zimbardo recruited several college students to recreate a prison in order to observe prisoner-guard behavior. As the study progressed, students playing the role of guard started abusing their fellow prisoners. Students playing the role of prisoner started revolting and protesting their treatment. After the sixth day, the study was so out of control, Zimbardo had to shut it down.[28] At the time, this was a landmark study. It gave evidence to the power of roles and situation upon moral behavior. Zimbardo concluded, given the right circumstances, people put aside their moral sense in order to fulfill a role.

However, serious flaws in the way these studies were carried out have now been pointed out. For example, in the Zimbardo study, researchers reviewing the study realized the recruitment process attracted a certain type of

---

[28] It is important to note such studies are now regarded as inhumane. The legal and ethical guidelines for psychological studies have become more stringent. Social scientists are held to higher standards today. The only studies approved by Institutional Review Boards (IRB's) are ones that do no physical or psychological harm to its subjects.

person with a particular subset of traits. These people tended to be more aggressive, narcissistic, and socially dominant. They believed in authoritarian leadership, had no qualms with manipulation, and rated low on an empathy and altruism scale. Researchers concluded that the catastrophic results of the study had nothing to do with the roles or situation, but had everything to do with the values, intent and character of the participants. In other words, it was what the subjects brought to the study that made the roles appear so evil, not the roles themselves.

As for the Milgram studies, there were also serious flaws in the research design. The study reported 65% of people kept administering the shocks, which is a misleading percentage. 65% is the result from one of 21 variations of the same study. In other variations, many people resisted the order to administer a lethal shock. They did so early and often. When all the studies are taken together, a surprising result emerges. The more subjects were ordered to administer the shocks, the more they resisted and the less they carried it out. Those who did administer the shocks to lethal levels did so not because of an order, but because of an internal struggle. Subjects chose to administer lethal shocks when the experimenter exhorted them to do it for the sake of science. Therefore, the study actually shows the opposite conclusion to what was originally purported. People didn't blindly obey an authority figure, but they did make morally questionable choices when they thought it served a higher purpose, such as advancing science.

Therapy for Teth

Let's pretend Black Adam reflects on his own moral nature and is confused. He's baffled by his own actions. His motivations are unclear to him and he wants to know definitively if he's good or bad. Social science shows us that evil is not defined by situations, roles or obedience to authority. Evil has to do with the particular characteristics of an individual and what their beliefs are. Hitler thought he was doing the world a great service by eradicating it of an inferior race, namely the Jews. People followed Hitler and were willing to commit morally atrocious deeds because they believed in his message. His followers carried out horrible deeds because they thought it served a greater purpose. Therefore, the *why* mattered more than the *what*. What (genocide, war, murder) doesn't matter when it achieves the why (pure race, dominance, revenge).

As for Teth-Adam, I think it's clear that he justifies his actions, good or bad, in the attempt of gaining power. When he first received power from Shazam, something shifted. The good persona or façade melted away. The true character of Teth-Adam emerged. He believes any action at any cost, if it produces the end goal of more power, is acceptable. I would share my observation with Black Adam. He may not see a problem with that kind of thinking. If so, I would challenge him to think deeper. Why does he love power so much? At what cost is power gained? His pursuit of power has led to the death of at least 2 million lives, including the death of his wife and brother. What good is power if everyone around is dead? Hopefully, Black Adam would count the cost and realize power simply isn't worth it. "What good will it be for someone to gain the whole world, yet forfeit their soul?"[29]

The fact of the matter is that we all do this to one extent or another. We all justify bad

---

[29] Matthew 16:26b, NIV.

behavior if it gets us our goal. We cheat on our taxes because we want more money. We misrepresent our children's achievements because we want them to get into a good college. We use addictive substances to escape uncomfortable feelings. And so, evil is truly faced with the tradeoffs of life. Evil rears its ugly head by offering us our desires, but through unethical or illegal means.

Virtue, one could say, is the pursuit of the same goal, but without the shortcut. Virtue is the denial of the tradeoff. That is the dividing line between Black Adam and, say, Captain Marvel or Superman. They want happiness, peace and power just like Black Adam, but they refuse to achieve those goals through any means possible. They are patient, even if the goal is never achieved. So, ask yourself next time you really want something and you are tempted to cut a corner, is the tradeoff really worth it? If you do cut the corner, are you any better than Black Adam?

Scarlet Witch

Gypsy, orphan, witch, mutant, super-villain, superhero—Scarlet Witch takes the gamut when it comes to tragedies, powers, roles and allegiances. Wanda, along with her twin brother Pietro, was the product of Magneto and Magda's union.

If you remember back to the Magneto chapter, Magneto lost his first daughter in a tragic fire, and then left his wife without any knowledge of her pregnancy with twins. Magda gave birth at Mount Wundagore, home to the High Evolutionary. Again, if you remember from the Warlock chapter, the High Evolutionary was a scientist who developed the power to evolve or devolve himself or others. Okay, back to the story.

The High Evolutionary kidnaps the twins, keeping them in stasis for several years. The children are eventually placed in the care of two gypsies, Django and Marya Maximoff. To make a long story short, the twins discover their powers; their family's encampment is attacked, resulting in the death Marya; they flee to a nearby town, Wanda accidentally burns down a house, villagers want to kill them, they are rescued by Magneto, they feel indebted to him and subsequently join his Brotherhood of Mutants without knowing he's their biological father... Phew! That was mouthful.

After some time, the twins take on the persona of the Scarlet Witch and Quicksilver. Disenchanted with Magneto's agenda, the twins leave his Brotherhood for the Avengers. While in the Avengers, Scarlet Witch meets the Vision, an android created by Ultron to destroy the Avengers. (The Vision turned against his creator and joined the Avengers team). The two fall in love and marry. Now, you may be thinking, "Wait a second. A human woman (female mutant, to be accurate) falls in love and marries a robot?" You're right to be confused; however, you have to understand that Vision is no ordinary android.

He's an android with a, for lack of a better term, soul. He has feelings. He can make moral choices. He can even rebel against his evil creator and switch sides. And, Scarlet Witch was able to use a hex so that they could reproduce. The couple has two sons, William and Thomas. So, it's not that crazy.

Sadly, their marital bliss is short-lived. In a series of attacks from super-villains, Vision's mind and body are taken over, paralyzed, and dismantled, necessitating Dr. Hank Pym to reassemble Vision, but without his soul. The original brain patterns of the Vision are lost, even his synthetic skin is different. This is an incredible loss for the Scarlet Witch. Think about it, when Vision was dismantled, Scarlet Witch essentially lost her husband. The android body remained, but whom she knew her spouse to be was no longer.

To compound Scarlet Witch's misery, she finds out that her sons are actually fragments of the demon Mephisto. Through a series of events, the two boys reintegrate with the demon. In other words, her two sons no longer exist, they died. As if losing her husband wasn't enough, Scarlet Witch had to deal with the loss of her kids.

Understandably, she temporarily goes insane, forcing her and her recovering husband to separate. The two go to different Avenger teams to get some distance. Eventually, Vision starts regaining his "soul" by adopting new brain patterns. He tries to patch things up with his wife, but nothing seems to work.

Sympathy for Scarlet

Imagine the Scarlet Witch and Vision walk into my office hoping to give their relationship one last chance. I would start by pointing out that the Vision has suffered a "traumatic brain injury" (TBI), to put it in human terms. That type of injury can result in memory impairment. In fact, Scarlet Witch and Vision's story isn't that far off from a real-life story. In 2012, a movie called *The Vow*, starring Channing Tatum and Rachel McAdams, was released. In a nutshell, the story was about a young couple, madly in love and recently married, enduring a nightmarish accident. The two were struck by an oncoming car while driving. Paige, played by McAdams, suffers a TBI and doesn't remember her husband or marriage at all. She looks at him, but feels nothing. Leo, played by Tatum, is dogged in his love for Paige. He eventually woos, romances and marries his wife all over again. Ah, isn't love great! Now, before you roll your eyes, understand that this is a true story. Leo and Paige are real people (their real names are Kim and Krickitt Carpenter). Needless to say, there's hope for Scarlet and her husband yet.

I would explain Kim and Krickitt's story to the couple to give them some context for what happened to them. Vision isn't going to bounce back from his TBI automatically. It's going to take some time and Wanda needs to be patient. In a manner of speaking, they are practically a newlywed couple all over again. That means they need to establish (more like reestablish) healthy relational patterns of communicating, forgiving, fighting, and responding to each other. Vision will regain feelings, but that doesn't mean they'll instantly have a perfect relationship. Relationships take work and effort. Consequently, I have outlined relational keys for building a better marriage that I would walk them through:

- **Listen to Understand – Not to Build Counterarguments.** I've recently started the habit of asking myself this very important question: "Am I listening to my wife in order to understand her, or am I just building ammunition for my own argument?" Ask yourself this question, and come back to reality. Nothing ever gets resolved if neither party is listening in a meaningful attempt to understand the other person's perspective.

- **Choose your Battles.** This one sounds tired and overused — but oh man, will it save your bacon! Simply put, some battles don't need to be fought. When you're not sure what to do, ask yourself two questions: "Am I more invested in winning this battle than my spouse is? And if I'm not, can I simply just trust my spouse with this issue?" Learn to trust your spouse's judgment, whether you totally agree or not. Sometimes, losing the battles helps you win the war (not that marriage is a war).

- **Make Apologies — without Qualifications.** I learned this the hard way. When I used to apologize to my wife for mistakes, I would often couch my apologies in all the reasons why I did what I did. Don't apologize while simultaneously trying to justify your actions. This is not a true, authentic apology. When apologizing, remove the word "but" from your vocabulary. Actually own up to what you did, understand how your actions affected the other person, and make amends.

- **Take Ownership for your Actions.** This may come as a surprise, but you are not perfect! You have no one to blame for your actions but yourself. You control you. Regardless of how your spouse acts, you are ultimately responsible for how you behave. Stop blaming your spouse for your actions and reactions. Take ownership.

- **Replace Judgments with Feedback on Behavior.** When giving feedback to your spouse, some of the worst things you can say are, "You, liar!" or "You're irrational, selfish, irresponsible..." We all want to say these things, but it never ends well. Why? Because these things are labels— judgments of one's character. They are meant to damage, not clarify or help. Instead, give your spouse feedback on his or her behavior, and how that behavior affected you.

- **Be Flexible.** If you didn't want to change, you shouldn't have gotten married! Marriage is the laboratory of life. It is the place where you try new things, make mistakes and learn valuable lessons. You cannot *not* be changed by it. So, let marriage do its work. If you won't change for your spouse, who would you change for? Who better to change for than your spouse?

- **Assume the Best.** I've made the mistake of holding on to my wife's past mistakes. Each time a new issue arises, all past mistakes come flooding to my mind, giving an added intensity to every fight. I jump to conclusions, thinking she's "messed up again." Such behavior simply isn't fair. And it predisposes a couple to look only for the negative. Assuming the best of your spouse sets you up for success and helps you see all the positives.

- **Becoming the Right Person, Not Being the Right Person.** Marriage isn't about finding the "right person." The right person is a myth. There is no perfect person out there for you. Reality bears a different truth. You find a person that you can love; a person that is worthy of changing for. And that person will require changes of you that will make you a better person, not a person under their control or of their design. Marriage is a process of becoming. You grow into the person you aim to be. You grow into the couple you aim to be. Great couples are made, not born.

I would share and process each marriage key with the couple. But insight isn't enough. Scarlet Witch and Vision need an experience of each concept. I would have them bring up a topic of conflict and then referee as they use some of the concepts we've covered. I want them to practice the ideas, then use them at home. Practice makes perfect. I would also recommend they give each other an extra dose of grace. Trying new things, learning new relational patterns, is hard work. They're bound to make mistakes. Yet, if they can respond to each other's mistakes with grace, it will make the learning process safe and enjoyable.

If you find yourself needing couples counseling, please don't wait. Couples have a tendency to delay seeking help. On average, couples seek help seven years after a problem has begun.[30] The consequence of waiting can be dire. Seven years allows a relational problem to incubate and grow into an intractable problem. In other words, waiting sets you up for failure. Don't make this mistake. Early intervention is the best possible choice. At the risk of sounding repetitive, seek help early!

---

[30] https://www.gottman.com/blog/timing-is-everything-when-it-comes-to-marriage-counseling/. Retrieval: January, 22nd, 2016.

Hulk

Robert Bruce Banner, the Incredible Hulk, nuclear physicist, Avenger—you know, the big green angry guy in shredded purple pants. The Hulk is indestructible, unimaginably strong and has a bit of a temper. How did a nuclear physicist become the Hulk?

Robert Bruce Banner, who goes by Bruce Banner, was the son of atomic physicist Brian Banner, who worked on creating clean nuclear energy. Yet, all was not right in the Banner home. That Bruce had a "rough childhood" is an understatement. His father was an angry alcoholic who hated his son. Bruce's mother tried compensating with extra affection, but this only intensified Brian's rage. Things got so bad, Brian one day killed his wife and threatened his son should he ever tell. Bruce didn't say a word out of fear. It was Brian's boasting about the murder that landed him in a psychiatric ward. Therefore, one could say, Bruce Banner was born out of rage.

After essentially losing both his parents, life didn't get much better for young Bruce. He was picked on by kids at school. He struggled with mental health issues. And developing relationships was difficult for the young man; he only had one true friendship. The bullying got so bad, Bruce planted a fake bomb at his school and threatened to blow everyone up. After police arrived they discovered the bomb was a fake – Bruce was expelled from school. There was one silver lining from the incident: the military noticed the talent of the young bomb-maker. They kept their eyes on his progress. Later, Bruce earned a doctorate in nuclear physics and began a career with the military.

While supervising gamma bomb experiments for the U.S. Defense Department, a young man wanders into the testing site right before they trigger a gamma bomb. Banner rushes in, pushes the young man out of the way and takes the full force of the blast. His body is irradiated with deadly gamma rays, yet he somehow survives... with a few side effects. Whenever Banner became overly excited, he would transform into a mindless, monstrous green beast. That was one of the Hulk manifestations. Another was a smaller (relative to the enormous green Hulk) grey Hulk who would only appear at night. At one time the grey Hulk took over Banner completely and worked as a bouncer in Las Vegas. The multiple personas became a problem. A battle for dominance was waged in Banner's subconscious. Banner was forced to work through his unresolved feelings regarding his alcoholic father. The end product was a unified green Hulk. He had the mind of Bruce Banner and the body of green Hulk. He was called "the Professor." Sadly, Hulk would not remain in this harmonious state. The rage side of Hulk would reemerge.

I would like to offer a few side notes before diving into the help-for-Hulk section. Initially, it was adrenaline that would initiate the emergence of Hulk, not anger. Then it became anger that initiated Banner's transformation into the Hulk. It's important to differentiate adrenaline and anger since the two are not the same. Adrenaline is a stress hormone produced and released by a biological system that underlies many feelings, responses and aspects of our day-to-day experience. In many cases, adrenaline can be useful if not necessary for survival. Adrenaline energizes us for the tasks of the day, alerts us to danger, motivates us to act, and marshals all our resources when faced with a challenge. However, there is a down side to adrenaline. States of prolonged adrenaline can become harmful.

Writers changed the cause of Banner's transformation into the Hulk from adrenaline to anger.[31] This created a new motif for the story. Anger connects with Banner's back story considering he had a raging alcoholic father. Also, adrenaline is involved in many experiences that people encounter on a daily basis, whereas anger is more contained. If Banner transformed into the Hulk every time adrenaline hit his system, he'd be turning into the Hulk all the time. Humans have stress all the time, but anger is an emotion, connected with the stress response, but that is

---

[31] Adrenaline is released when people have sex, exercise, watch movies, ride bicycles, play sports, give performances and so on. It is a normal, daily part of human experience. Banner would be constantly turning into the Hulk if he transformed every time adrenaline was released in his body. Therefore, it makes more sense to change the cause of his transformation from adrenaline to anger. Also, anger fits better with Banner's back story.

triggered only on occasion. Hopefully, I didn't lose you there. So, what if Banner or his chilled-out big, green self, walked into my office seeking help on how to control anger?

Help for Hulk

To get a better understanding of where Banner is coming from, it's important to know why he spends a considerable amount of time and energy trying to avoid the raging green Hulk. When green Hulk takes over, he's easily manipulated (enemies often use this weakness to their advantage). He has low intelligence, is constantly in a destructive rage, and causes incredible amounts of damage. And his rage can be, but isn't necessarily, blind – meaning, he will attack friend or foe. There's nothing jolly about this green giant! You can see why Banner would like to avoid the green Hulk at all costs.

Is there any correlation between real life and the rage our storied Hulk experiences? Apart from a normal, middle-aged man transforming into one of the most destructive beasts in the universe, yeah. It's a fairly accurate picture.

Rage is a form of extreme anger. Imagine an anger spectrum, with frustration on one end and rage on the other. Rage is the point at which a person has lost control. The anger is now calling the shots. For example, further along in the story Banner is separated from the green Hulk. This is a disastrous choice, though. The Hulk (minus Banner) is a near-mindless, raging beast. Turns out, when they were merged together, Banner's consciousness was able to exert some control. Green Hulk without Banner's influence is more raging, more destructive, and more mindless than ever before. Banner is forced to reintegrate with the green beast to act as a floodgate for his rage. So, what are the costs and benefits of anger? And how are the Hulk, and you, supposed to control anger instead of letting it control you?

The Benefits of Anger

Anger has been thought of as a substitute emotion. Suppose you are feeling vulnerable, and you don't feel comfortable processing those feelings. You can choose to substitute that feeling with anger as a way to protect yourself. This can be very healthy when done in the right context and time. It can also be very destructive when in the wrong context and time (but more on that in the next section).

Furthermore, if you are having an excess of emotional pain, anger can be an effective distraction. People do all sorts of harmful things when they are ill-equipped to deal with intense, overwhelming emotional pain. Some turn to illicit addictive substances like cocaine, heroin or methamphetamine. Others will self-harm, like cutting, cigarette burning or self-choking. And even others engage in risk-taking behavior like driving recklessly, getting into physical altercations, acting out sexually or overspending via shopping or gambling. Therefore, you could make the argument, if getting really angry distracts you from engaging in any one of the listed vices, then go for it.

Additionally, anger can motivate you to address a problem or grievance. Anger has a way of animating people to action. Feeling sad, anxious, overwhelmed, and fearful can paralyze you. But anger will do the opposite. It gives you the momentum to say the things you are afraid to say. It allows you to voice an uncomfortable opinion and stand up for yourself and others. In this sense, productive anger could be the cure for anesthetized masses. You could say we don't feel anger enough. We see a problem, and instead of getting angry and doing something about it, we accept the problem as-is. We become inoculated to action.

The Costs of Anger

On the flipside of anger as a substitute emotion, it is certainly possible to overprotect. If you never allow yourself to feel vulnerability, you're essentially shackling yourself. That vulnerable feeling needs to be addressed. Metaphorically speaking, anger can be a prison—you have become so afraid of addressing how you really feel that the instant your feelings hit you, whatever the vulnerable feeling is, you run to the safety of anger. This can really harm you and your relationships. Let's say your spouse raises an issue in your relationship. You know she's right, but you don't want to admit that, because it has implications that could damage your ego. So instead of engaging in an honest, meaningful conversation, you lash out. The results of doing this aren't good.

The Center for Disease Control and Prevention (CDC) has stated 85% of all diseases have a strong link to your emotional state.[32] That means how you feel has an impact on your physical health. Sustained, chronic anger wrecks your health. Angry people live shorter, unhealthier and unhappier lives. Prolonged and unmanaged anger can result in headaches, digestion problems, insomnia, increased anxiety, depression, high blood pressure, skin problems, increased risk for heart attack and stroke.[33]

Furthermore, when anger gets to the point of rage, you are no longer in control. Neurologically speaking, the resources available to your brain are limited. Rage has a way of dominating everything else. I've worked with many clients who have said and done things they sorely regret after a bout of anger. Rage siphons all the resources away from the parts of your brain responsible for impulse control, critical thinking, and analysis. When operating from a resource deficit like that, you are merely reacting to

---

[32] Better Health: https://www.betterhealth.vic.gov.au/health/healthyliving/anger-how-it-affects-people. Retrieval: January, 26th, 2016.
[33] Everyday Health: http://www.everydayhealth.com/news/ways-anger-ruining-your-health/. Retrieval: January, 26th, 2016.

whatever is said or done around you. Needless to say, you aren't functioning at your best because you aren't in control. You aren't making choices.

How to Control Anger

We've covered the positives and negatives of anger, but how do you put yourself in control? Many people try ineffective methods of controlling their anger which stand cross-purposed to their goals. Ineffective strategies like blowing up or bottling-up tend to intensify anger. So, here are a few suggestions on how to control anger:

- **Proper Self-Care**: Regular exercise, doing something you enjoy (like a hobby), spending time with friends and family, gardening, meditation, taking a vacation and a healthy diet all aid in sustaining emotional health. Self-care can soothe, distract, and diffuse rage.
- **Time-Outs**: Giving yourself time to cool off can decrease the intense feelings of anger and allow your brain resources to be reallocated to areas responsible for impulse control and critical thinking. This

will give you time to think and evaluate instead of simply reacting.

- **Perspective**: See the whole picture. Anger has positives and negatives; it isn't always bad. This perspective will enable you to make wise choices. Sometimes it is appropriate to express your anger. Sometimes it is appropriate to allow your anger to propel you to action. Other times, cooler heads prevail. The trick is distinguishing between those appropriate and inappropriate times.

- **Outlets**: Sometimes you just need to vent. In this case, call a friend, go out to drinks with a co-worker or do a project with a family member and let it out. Let loose that pent up frustration in a healthy avenue. Doing something physical, to get your frustration out, can be incredibly helpful as well. Go for a hike, play basketball, get a run in.

- **Self-Understanding**: Anger is a response to something; it doesn't happen without a reason. If you can do the hard work of understanding what triggers your anger, you will be better prepared. Having an understanding and strategy for your triggers will put you in control.

- **Express Anger without Attacking**: Being angry is a normal aspect of life. Expressing anger is a normal aspect of life. But some do it better than others. Some allow their anger to be a justification to viciously attack another. This is not okay. Being angry doesn't give license to have a tantrum, be cruel to others or communicate poorly. Share your feelings, but don't attack others.

I would encourage Banner not to avoid his anger, but to embrace it. Being angry is normal; it's impossible to avoid. And I would say the same to you. Anger is used as a justification for running away from vulnerability, attacking others, or feeding an addiction. Don't let that be you. Don't be the Hulk. Control your anger, don't let it control you.

Spectre

stral Avenger, Spirit of Redemption and Vengeance, Aztar; otherwise known as Spectre, possibly the strongest superhero in the DC universe. Wait, what? What about Superman, Black Adam or Hulk? Sorry, Spectre trumps them all. The reason being, Spectre is an incarnation or aspect of the Presence. The Presence is DC's representation of God. This may be a bit confusing, so let me give you an example. In the big three monotheistic world religions— Christianity, Judaism, and Islam— God has different attributes such as omnipotence, omniscience, perfect moral character, things like that. Yet, in the big three, all God's different characteristics are unified—much like you may have different characteristics, but you're still a person with one identity. However, this is not the case with the Presence. The Presence has different characteristics manifesting as their own identity, and that's where the Spectre comes in. The Spectre is the Presence's wrath and vengeance. He inflicts punishment upon sinful people. What is interesting about Spectre, he wasn't always an incarnation of God's wrath. He was at one time an angel. In fact, he was an angel that rebelled against God with Lucifer.

As the story goes, Aztar, which was his name at the time, followed Lucifer and was expelled from God's presence. Yet, Aztar had a change of heart and repented of his sins and returned to God. God forgave Aztar, yet he stripped the angel of his memory and transformed him into the Spectre. Spectre executes God's divine judgments upon man. He's responsible for the destruction of Sodom and Gomorrah, the ten plagues against Egypt, splitting the Red Sea and tumbling the walls of Jericho. Yet, when Jesus was incarnated as a man, walked this Earth and ministered, God's love and vengeance (Spectre) couldn't be in proximity. So, he was banished to Limbo until the Crucifixion of Christ. Following Christ's death and resurrection,

Spectre was set free to exact God's vengeance on a day called "Dies Irae" or *Day of Wrath*.

Spectre unleashed a torrent of judgment, but the Archangel Michael informed Spectre that his freedom was limited to inhabiting a dead body. At first, Spectre didn't want to follow the new rule, but he had no choice. Spectre would inhabit many bodies, but his first host proved the most problematic. Spectre inhabited a Hindu man named Caraka. Spectre has the ability to merge with his hosts. He doesn't "take-over" them. The two share the same body and mission from the Presence. The host has to decide to participate in the mission, but they usually go along with it because they're dead and the mission provides an opportunity to enact revenge on their killers. Yet, Caraka didn't make for a good host. Spectre's inhabitation interrupted his cycle of reincarnation. He was eager for any way out. Along came Sekuba, a succubus demon, who persuaded Caraka to expel Spectre and join him. He agreed. This new union formed Spectre's greatest enemy, known as Azmodus.

Spectre moved on to another host, Jim Corrigan, a New York City cop murdered by a mobster. Once Spectre inhabits Corrigan, he metes out justice against the mobster. Corrigan returns to life, kills the mobsters and saves his fiancé. Later on, he associated with the Minuteman and eventually joined the Justice Society of America. Spectre goes on to have many hosts and does many great things, including saving Earth and the universe more than once (and occasionally endangering it, too). But his story revolves around this one theme: justice.

Sympathy for Spectre

Spectre's cause is righteous and moral, but keep in mind, he was originally a rebelling angel. After the rebellion led by Lucifer ended Aztar repented of his sins and returned to the Presence. What happens next is very interesting. The Presence wipes clean Aztar's memory and gives him a new name, Spectre. Spectre is, at this point, *tabula rasa*, meaning he is a "blank slate." The term and the meaning behind it has a longstanding history in the field of philosophy. The philosophical idea is that people aren't born with innate knowledge of things like morality. That, in fact, people are products of their environment, upbringing, and training. Tabula rasa is entangled with the centuries old debate of *nature versus nurture*. The tabula rasa camp strongly argues for nurture being the primary shaping force in a person's life. Whereas those in the nature camp strongly argue that people are born with innate knowledge like morality.

How does tabula rasa and nature versus nurture have anything to do with Spectre? When Aztar rebelled and repented, the Presence made him a blank slate when he removed his memory. Then, the Presence gives Spectre a new mission. He is to be God's instrument of justice. He is to mete out punishment on the wicked. But here's the real question, can the Presence shape Spectre into a moral being by forcing him to be moral? Remember, Spectre was forced into the role of God's vengeance. He initially resisted.

In order to answer the questions above we must step back and ask a more fundamental question, is morality a learned trait? Or is it innate? There may, in fact, be a biological component to morality. Paul Bloom, a psychologist at the Infant Cognition Center at Yale University, conducted a study analyzing the moral impulses of infants. In one study, he demonstrated that infants, even as young as six months, had a preference for someone helping a person in need. He also showed that infants possessed a preference for the punishment of someone who harmed another person.[34] It would seem there is a genetic factor to morality. We are hardwired to help those in need and punish those who do wrong.

Moral Stages

Lawrence Kohlberg, a psychologist and pioneer in the area of moral development, would say this moral impulse in infants is actually the first stage of many. He formulated a three-level, six-stage process that children pass through:

- Level 1: Pre-conventional Morality
  - Stage 1. Obedience and punishment orientation.
  - Stage 2. Naively egoistic orientation.
- Level 2: Conventional Morality
  - Stage 3. Good boy orientation.
  - Stage 4. Authority and social order maintaining orientation.

---

[34] The New York Times: http://www.nytimes.com/2010/05/09/magazine/09babies-t.html?_r=0. Retrieval: January, 28th, 2016.

- Level 3: Post-Conventional Morality
    - o Stage 5. Contractual legalistic orientation.
    - o Stage 6. Conscience or principle orientation.[35]

His stage model works like this "Kohlberg views the six stages as forming an invariant developmental sequence in which attainment of an advanced stage is dependent on the attainment of each of the preceding stages. It is further assumed that a more advanced stage is not simply an addition to a less advanced stage, but represents a reorganization of less advanced levels."[36] In certain periods of life, stages may overlap each other and one stage may take longer to develop than expected. Each child needs to be viewed as an individual: these stages are not standards, but more like landmarks of healthy development. Unfortunately, we can't get into the details of each stage, yet there is considerable

---

[35] Kohlberg, Lawrence (1967). The development of children's orientation toward order: Sequence in the development of moral thought. Vista Humana, 6, 11-33.
[36] Rest, J.; Turiel, E.; Kohlberg, L. (1969). Level of Moral Development as a Determinant of Preference and Comprehension of Moral Judgments made by Others. *Journal of Personality*, 37(2), 225.

evidence that children do pass through stages as they morally develop.

Moral Thinking

From a cognitive perspective, it is evident that children are actively thinking through a right-and-wrong lens in regards to their actions and the actions of others. This suggests that children are not blank tablets in which their parent's ideas and standards of morality are simply imprinted. Children reason their way through mom and dad's moral lens, and then act on their own conclusions. McDevitt et al. (2004) said, "Some [children] are quite critical of how the preceding generation behaves and insist on behaving differently."[37] This gives evidence to the idea that children are actively processing the moral landscape of their culture, generation and personal experience.

---

[37] McDevitt, Teresa M. & Ormrod, Jeanne Ellis (2004). Child Development: Educating and Working with Children and Adolescents, 2nd Ed. Upper Saddle River, New Jersey: Pearson Education, Inc. p. 435.

Moral Feeling

Other theorists have postulated that children base their reasoning on the emotional aspect of right and wrong. [38] They see a correlation between positive emotions and making a morally acceptable decision, and negative emotions related with making morally wrong decisions. Based on this theory, children will make *prosocial* decisions because it feels good.[39] In other words, it feels good to do what is good.

Moral Parenting

But what about the parents? What role do they play in their kid's moral development? Adolescents who have a good relationship with their parents and a strong sense of community service have a greater likelihood to grow up to be morally conscientious and generative adults. Yet, that moral framework in adolescence is built

---

[38] Aronfreed, J. (1976). Moral Development from the Standpoint of a General Psychological Theory. T. Lickona (Ed.) Moral Development and Behavior: Theory, Research and Social Issues. Pp. 54-69.

[39] McDevitt, Teresa M. & Ormrod, Jeanne Ellis (2004). Child Development: Educating and Working with Children and Adolescents, 2nd Ed. Upper Saddle River, New Jersey: Pearson Education, Inc. p. 436.

upon what they learned in early childhood. Hart and Carlo (2005) have pointed out how the moral experiences one has in childhood shape the moral experience one has adolescence. [40] In fact, the relationship between parent and child can enhance or blunt a child's moral sense. A study done by Grazyna Kochanska (1991) found that "Parental discipline that deemphasizes the use of power, and thus presumably capitalizes on the child's internal arousal associated with wrongdoing, results in more intense feelings of discomfort."[41] Kochanska observed that children of parents who use love and sympathy with their children fostered a stronger sense of internal guilt when being corrected for bad behavior. Alternatively, children of parents who use aggressive and forceful actions develop a stronger sense of external consequences rather than

---

[40] Hart, Daniel & Carlo, Gustavo (2005). Moral Development in Adolescence. Journal of Research of Adolescence, 15 (3), 223-233.

[41] Kochanska, Grazyna (1991). Socialization and Temperament in the Development of Guilt and Conscience. Child Development, National Institute of Mental Health, 62, 1379-1392.

internal. Hart and Carlo (2005) remarked that "adolescence is the foundation for adulthood."[42]

Morality and Anxiety

Kochanska also observed that children with anxiety levels have a stronger moral orientation than children without such high levels of anxiety. These children who don't have high anxiety need different parenting practices applied to them. It seems that anxiety heightens our moral sense. We analyze our choices and the choices of others more when anxious, as opposed to being less conscientious of our moral choices, the implications of them and the moral choices of others when we are calm. A good dose of anxiety may boost your moral life.

Morality and Mental Health

Hopefully, the information provided above is sufficient for answering those two fundament questions: is morality a learned trait? Or is it innate? As you can see, morality is genetic,

---

[42] Hart, Daniel & Carlo, Gustavo (2005). Moral Development in Adolescence. Journal of Research of Adolescence, 15 (3), 223-233.

developmental, cognitive, emotive, heightened by anxiety and influenced by parents. Therefore, morality is innate and it is learned. It is natural to be, crave and work towards moral ends. Morality is an essential part of being human.[43] *We are most healthy when we are living morally congruent lives.*

Now, we can answer the question regarding Spectre. Can the Presence shape the Spectre into a moral being by *making* him be moral? Yes, and no. Spectre isn't a blank slate, no one is. People are innately moral, but, that innate morality is dependent upon moral training. Healthy moral development involves *nature* AND *nurture*. Therefore, the problem isn't that the Presence can shape the Spectre into a moral being, that he can do and it will work. The problem is that he going to *force* the Spectre to be moral by not giving in a choice. The *how* matters; one's *approach* is of critical importance. Aggressive and forceful parents can actually do harm to their children's moral development. Yet, the involved, engaged parent who has moral expectations, which is accompanied by support is far more successful. Expectations plus support

---

[43] Psychology bears this truth out as do the Judeo-Christian and Muslim worldviews.

has the best outcomes, and in that regard, the Presence is wrong. From this perspective, Spectre is a moral instrument, but not a moral agent. He is merely a slave carrying out the will of his master.

Your Moral Growth

The moral path may, at times, be difficult to follow. Whoever said doing what's right is going to be easy? Or for that matter, whoever said doing what is meaningful would be easy? Even though you know you should do what is right, it can be really hard to do. I would challenge Spectre and you to embrace the difficulty. Rid yourself of the false assumption that doing what's right and pursuing meaning will always be easy. It won't. But, it will always be worth the pain.

For those who have moral convictions, but aren't living in accordance with them, you are intentionally leading yourself into a state of *cognitive dissonance.* If you remember, cognitive dissonance is the psychological state of your beliefs not matching your actions. This is not a fun place to be in. I would recommend resolving this before it carries on too long. Seek out a friend, mentor, pastor, priest, Imam and share what you are thinking and feeling. It can't hurt to receive sage counsel from a trusted advisor.

For those of you who don't think live by a moral standard or code, I would argue that you actually do; you just aren't aware of it. It could be helpful if you investigated the standards, codes and worldview that you live by. Gaining more awareness of the thoughts and beliefs that govern how you respond, interpret and make decisions is a very psychologically healthy thing to do. Walk through the different factors that shape morality mentioned in this chapter and ask yourself what Kohlberg stage are you in? What did your parents teach you about morality? What kind of moral lives did they live? What do you think about the moral issues of the day? What do you feel when you do something you know to be wrong? How do you feel when someone acts immoral towards you? Doing this allows you to be more intentional with how you live. It gives your life a sense of purpose and direction when needing to make choices. And, if everyone is living a moral lifestyle, wouldn't the world become a better place? What's good for you is good for the world. So, live a morally congruent life and you will be happier.

Epilogue

Hopefully, you enjoyed this little jaunt into the world of superheroes, counseling and psychology. You've learned about superheroes, super-villains, the DC and Marvel universes, psychology and counseling, but most importantly, you've learned something about yourself. Comic book characters, like I said in the introduction, are reflections of humanity. When we look in the mirror of comics, we see the best and worst of ourselves. The benefit of reading comics is a self-distancing effect. What I mean is that when a character excels or struggles with something that relates to you, you are then provided with enough distance to analyze. Whereas, without the self-distancing, you are a fish in water, so to speak: you don't have an awareness of the very water you are swimming in. But what if a fish could leap on land and breathe? That would provide them with the opportunity to reflect on where they are: "Oh yeah, I'm a fish, and I live in water." Comics allow you to jump out of your "water" and look back at it: "Oh yeah, I have trauma in my past that I've never dealt with" "Huh? That's weird. I never noticed I use anger to distract myself from vulnerable feelings." Do yourself a favor and ask which comic book character or storyline connects with you the most. Then ask yourself *why*. What makes you love or hate them? Comics are not only entertainment. They can have tremendous personal value.

Appendix A

In this book, we have looked at individual stories from superheroes and supervillain alike in order to reflect upon human nature. But what about the big picture? What about the superhero story itself? The *metanarrative*—the *way* in which the superhero story is told—tell us something about ourselves. Is there something reflective of human nature in the way we conceive of the superhero? For starters, isn't it odd that in most superhero stories, the parents die? Speaking more broadly, there always seems to be loss somewhere in a superhero's background. Superman's parents and entire race died on Krypton. Batman's parents died during a mugging that went wrong. The Punisher's family was killed before his eyes. Spider-Man's parents were killed, along with Uncle Ben, Aunt May, Gwen Stacy, Harry Osborne, and Mary Jane (Spider-Man wins the "Dead Loved Ones" competition). Tony Stark's parents died when he was young. Scarlet Witch's dad abandoned her family right before her mom died while giving birth to her and her brother. I could easily fill this page with fictional superheroes' dead parents.

So, why is tragedy such an oft-used theme in the superhero narrative? We all have encountered loss and tragedy in our lives. Maybe you, too, have lost a parent. Needless to say, loss hurts. Loss has a way of paralyzing a person. However, loss doesn't have to lead to paralysis for the surviving loved ones. Loss can be overcome. Just because your parents, your uncle, your fiancé, or your best friend has died doesn't mean your life and future has died with them. You can carry on and live a fulfilling and meaningful life despite your loss.

In fact, loss and tragedy can be the engine of great things. Your pain can be transformative. It can shape you into a more compassionate, others-oriented person. Alternatively, it has the potential to make you a bitter and angry person, the kind of person who thinks the world owes them. Yet, the true "heroic" characteristic of superheroes is that they don't allow tragedy to embitter them. It deepens rather than shallows them. Superheroes become more conscientious of their fellow man rather than becoming more ego-driven and selfish.

Yet, the loss of a parent or loved one doesn't immunize superheroes against future challenges. Every superhero is challenged to their limits by an arch-enemy. A few examples are the Flash and the Reverse-Flash, Superman and Bizarro-Superman, Adam Warlock and the Magus, and Captain American and the Red Skull. The list goes on and on. But the idea is this: an arch-enemy is someone who rivals and parallels the superhero. The superhero could have become their arch-enemy had their choices been different. The supervillain allows the superhero to reflect on their choices and life path. It reinforces one essential truth that most can relate to: our choices matter. Our choices, not just the big ones, lead us down one direction or another. This is the one determinative factor in our lives. We cannot control what happens to us—what family or time or socio-economic status we were born into—but we can control our choices. And it is those choices that determine whether we become a hero or monster.

It is insightful to see how superheroes respond to their arch-enemies. Typically, arch-enemies know their superhero better than anyone else. They know their whole story, including their greatest triumphs, tragedies, whom they love, and what they are ashamed of. And, let's just say, arch-enemies don't handle this information delicately. In fact, they use every personal detail against the superhero. The death of Bruce Wayne's parents is brought up in nearly every comic book: either the Joker is taunting him about how he couldn't save his parents, or, like I mentioned in the Batman chapter, the Lump is attacking Batman psychologically with the deaths of his parents and sidekicks. But superheroes do something interesting when faced with their greatest weaknesses, failures, and traumas: they rise above it. Superheroes embrace their weaknesses and challenge themselves to become better.

Superheroes don't let past failures, loss, and tragedy stop them from making strides towards progress and growth. This is a powerful idea indeed for anyone wounded by tragedy. A personal failure does not equal defeat, and it is no excuse for not pursuing personal growth. Arch-enemies do superheroes a favor when they attack their weaknesses because they help the superhero identify the weakness and work towards resolution. Sometimes there is truth in criticism.

The superhero in you will take that critique as feedback and work towards becoming better.

As mentioned above, an arch-enemy can parallel, if not reflect, the superhero. Or, they show what the superhero could have become if they had made different decisions. Even though the superhero may not realize it, the arch-enemy because they are doing the superhero a favor. How exactly is the arch-enemy doing the superhero a favor? Every superhero, and every person for that matter, questions their decisions, especially if their decisions came with great sacrifice. Doubt is natural whenever a serious decision is made. But, doubt can also paralyze you from acting. The arch-enemy—by showing the superhero what an evil, ego-maniacal, selfish, and disastrous person they could have become— helps the superhero overcome their doubt. They make a true commitment to the path of goodness regardless of the cost. This is the "actualized self" of the superhero—a sacrificial commitment to their cause without regard to personal cost.

A real-life example is Nelson Mandela. Mandela was the leader of the African National Congress and was imprisoned by the oppressive government for nearly 28 years. The time in prison was brutal. Mandela's marriage suffered, he was denied contact with his kids, and, sadly, his oldest son died while he was in prison. Any other person would have been changed for the worse, but not Mandela. His suffering bettered him. When he was released from prison, his commitment to the cause of racial equality and a just system of government was stronger than ever. Nelson Mandela is a superhero in the flesh. He thrived when others would have only survived. He conquered injustice with compassion and an absolute commitment to what was right, even when that commitment came at great personal cost. Yet, Mandela was empowered to do what he did through the support of others.

This brings us to the topic of sidekicks. At one point or another, every superhero has a sidekick. Even Batman—lonely, lonely Batman—had four Robins. Other examples of superheroes with sidekicks are Iron Man and Warmachine, Wonder Woman and Wonder Girl, Adam Warlock and Pip the Troll, Doctor Strange and Wong, Superman and Jimmy Olsen—and one could argue that Batman and Superman are interchangeably each other's sidekicks. Even though each of these superheroes had amazing powers and abilities, they still needed a sidekick. I think the lesson here is obvious: two heads are better than one. You can't and shouldn't bear your burdens alone. Mankind was not made to live in isolation. You need sidekicks in your life. You need friends, co-workers, and family members who can support, encourage and inspire you. Life is hard. It doesn't mean you are weak if you need help from others.

Another interesting aspect of the superhero narrative arc is that most superheroes usually join a group of other superheroes. The Green Lantern Corps, Justice League of America, Teen Titans, Omega Men, the Watchmen, the Avengers, Guardians of the Galaxy, the X-Men: these are the most notable superhero groups, but there are many more. The fact that so many superheroes team up with others goes to show that superheroes need community. In this regard, again, superheroes are just like us. We all have a fundamental need to belong. It is not enough to have friends (sidekicks); we have an innate need to belong to a group. Why is that? Groups give an individual identity. When people describe themselves as "Mormons," "liberals," members of "the middle class," "gamers," "scientists," or "comic book fans," they are identifying with the groups they belong to. Belonging to a group gives identity, and identity gives meaning.

Every superhero has a different endowment of superpowers and abilities. From the power of flight to mental telepathy, superheroes have all kinds of superpowers. What is interesting about powers is that they aren't terribly useful until the superhero develops them. It took time for Doctor Strange to hone his powers. Through trial and error, he became Sorcerer Supreme. This isn't just true with superpowers, as human gifts and abilities operate in the same way. We are all given an assortment of gifts and abilities. You may not have X-ray vision, but maybe you are a gifted speaker, or good with language, or sensitive to the emotional states of others. Regardless of what your gifts and abilities are, learning is necessary for development. And in almost every superhero story, every superhero is faced with an important dilemma—will they risk failure in order to become the hero they are meant to be? The same dilemma will often face you. Will you risk pursuing a passion, or will you play it safe? Will you use your gifts and abilities for good purposes, or only to benefit yourself? Are you willing to be a superhero and use your passions, gifts, and talents to better those around you? That is the true test of a hero.

These are just a few observations regarding how comic book superheroes reflect the different aspects of human nature and can be instructive for your life. Ultimately, comic books are more than entertainment; they are a vehicle of discovery. They help us find the superhero inside of each one of us.

About the Author

Daniel Bates is a Licensed Mental Health Counselor who works with families dealing with violence, substance abuse and legal issues. He loves to write, think critically and drink coffee. He's passionate about writing and reading poetry, discussing philosophy/theology, spending time with his wife and daughters, connecting with friends and getting lost in a good book. He's fascinated by the intersection of faith/spirituality and mental health. He's written three books of poetry, a nonfiction book on the Christian mystics, and a self-help book on how to use the lessons life teaches us which are available on Amazon in Kindle and paperback. Daniel also writes for two online magazines: mum.info and FamilyShare.com in addition to his own blog. You can find links to Daniel's books, read his blog, and view and purchase his paintings at his website danielbates.co.

More from Daniel Bates

The Modern Mystic

 Wish your spiritual life wasn't mediocre? Is your prayer life dead? Are you jealous of the spiritual vitality that everyone else seems to have except for you? Don't let your life be ruled by a spiritual malaise. Instead of checking out, go further and deeper in to the heart of God.

But how?

The Christian mystics are ancient voices with a modern message. They teach that the love of God is deeper, wider and beyond anything you can understand. It is altogether mysterious and right in front of you. It is the paradoxical truth wrapped in the unimaginable love of a relational God eager to know and be known by you.

Yes, you are the object of God's love. And yes, God is the ultimate source of your happiness. Knowing and experiencing God's love will change you. Yet experiencing God's love is not a destination. It is a journey. And you are a sojourner in need of a guide. Allow the Christian mystics to direct you along the sometimes confusing wandering path of God's love.

When Parenting Backfires

Let's be honest. Parenting is hard. From the moment children take their first breaths, parents are faced with decisions and choices that no manual could ever fully explain. And the way you parent is constantly changing: babies need protection, toddlers need direction, and teens need influence. We as parents are simply expected to do it and do it well.

From two therapists who have a combined 25 years of experience working with families comes a new kind of parenting book. This book doesn't focus on technique, a discipline scheme or parenting style. This book focuses on the parent themselves, specifically the kind of thinking that makes parents effective or ineffective. In *When Parenting Backfires* examines 12 thinking errors commonly made by parents. In each chapter Dan and David:

- Explain the thinking error
- How it backfires
- What parents can do to correct the thinking error
- And real life examples of parents who have recognized their thinking error, made the correction, and improved their effectiveness.

Let this book do its work. Let down your guard and be open to the new ideas. As I've already said, the biggest risk you'll take is to your ego as you improve your parenting skills and your relationship with your kids. I think any effective parent is willing to take those odds. Are you?

Learning to Live

You are the reason you are stuck.

You can either stay stuck or learn how to get un-stuck. In order to get un-stuck, you must engage in the learning process. That means learning about yourself, your perceptions, your thinking, your communication style, and how you view relationships. But learning is hard to do with some help. Fortunately, an experienced therapist, Daniel Bates, has compiled 20 lessons based on his clinical experience and the latest social science research to help you.

Learning to Live will help you engage with the lifelong work of learning. Learning isn't an event, it's a journey. It can be painful, challenging at times and downright uncomfortable, but the end result is worth it. Lessons have a way of sticking with you for the rest of your life. They are the gift that keeps on giving. So, what are you waiting for? Start learning so you can start living.

Fatherhood, Despotism, and Mystical Mutterings

The late and great British journalist and writer G.K. Chesterton once said "We are perishing for want of wonder, not for want of wonders." We have remarkable technological advances, but what has all the progress done for us? We are jaded, and complacent. We have lost our ability to marvel, to wonder. And sadly, our ability to wonder and take joy has faded with all the pressures of life.

Poetry is an act of rebellion against a complacent life. Reading poetry makes us aware of the places worn thin between heaven and earth. It gives us a sense of transcendence and humanity, beauty and tragedy, joy and sorrow.

Fatherhood, Despotism, and Mystical Mutterings will make you will laugh, cry, think, be disturbed, elated, and ultimately, inspired to be creative yourself by reading this. Hopefully you may look beyond the mundanities of your life and find the divine through the power of the creative written word. And when you look up at the stars, you will marvel with ceaseless joy.

Mental Health Taxes

Poetry is an act of contrition. It's the art of looking at life in a painfully honest way. Poetry uses metaphors to capture life's intricate complications where plain, obvious and straightforward language fails.

This book explores those metaphors like the tax collector. Your difficult relationship is like an invisible tax collector on your mental health. Your stress is a mental health collector. Your fear of engaging with loss, pain, addiction, denial is your tax collector and it will keep collecting and collecting. Your mental health is taxed by what you avoid.

This is a work of art with the hidden agenda of helping you, art is subversive like that. Art without a purpose is just noise. The subversive purpose of this book is for you to engage with what you are most afraid to face. Embrace the discomfort. Become what life is shaping you into. Enjoy!

False Starts and Mishaps

Life is full of false starts and mishaps. But what's so great about how you start? Why do people care so much about where you come from, your family, what school you went to, do you have money? Shouldn't the focus be on how you use what you have?

And what's the deal with mishaps in life? A friend moves away, you lose your job, your kids don't respect you, loved one dies? Why do those things have to derail your life? These questions and more are explored in False Starts and Mishaps.

But isn't this a book of poetry? Shouldn't the book be about nature and flowers and babies or something? Poetry has a subversive agenda of trying to help with beautiful words, images and metaphors.

Podcasts and Blog from Daniel

Brainchild is a podcast for those who want to be entertained and informed. Brainchild goes deep into the latest research from psychology, the insights from counseling, and the personal experiences Daniel has accrued over his career. You can find Brainchild at brainchildpodcast.co on Podbean. You can also listen to Brainchild on Daniels' website, danielbates.co, and find blogs, books and more.

Daniel co-hosts a podcast with author and therapist David Simonsen, PhD. The podcast focuses on mental health, relational and emotional growth, and pop culture. Dan and David take calls from listeners with relational and mental health questions, they interview special guests, review movies and analyze the political landscape through the lens of a therapist.

Daniel's blog, videos, books, and information about counseling services can be found on his website, danielbates.co. In addition to his self-help material, you can learn more about Daniel's artistic interests. He's written three books of poetry and loves to paint. His poetry and paintings are featured on the website. New blogs, podcasts and videos are added to the site every week.

Counseling Services

If you are interested contacting Daniel for counseling, he recently expanded his private practice at Lacamas Counseling in Camas, Washington. You can find information about Daniel's counseling specialties, location of the office or other counselors that may be a fit for you at lacamascounseling.com. He's currently accepting new clients. Email or Call to schedule an appointment.

Lightning Source UK Ltd.
Milton Keynes UK
UKOW05f2015200217

294867UK00013B/144/P